Ted Bundy

The Terrifying True Crime Story of America's Most Notorious Serial Killer

**By
James Richmond**

© **Copyright 2021 - All rights reserved.**

The content contained within this book may not be reproduced, duplicated or transmitted without direct written permission from the author or the publisher.

Under no circumstances will any blame or legal responsibility be held against the publisher, or author, for any damages, reparation, or monetary loss due to the information contained within this book, either directly or indirectly.

Legal Notice:

This book is copyright protected. It is only for personal use. You cannot amend, distribute, sell, use, quote or paraphrase any part, or the content within this book, without the consent of the author or publisher.

Disclaimer Notice:

Please note the information contained within this document is for educational and entertainment purposes only. All effort has been executed to present accurate, up to date, reliable, complete information. No warranties of any kind are declared or implied. Readers acknowledge that the author is not engaging in the rendering of legal, financial, medical or professional advice. The content within this book has been derived from various sources. Please consult a licensed professional before attempting any techniques outlined in this book.

By reading this document, the reader agrees that under no circumstances is the author responsible for any losses, direct or indirect, that are incurred as a result of the use of information contained within this document, including, but not limited to, errors, omissions, or inaccuracies.

Table of Contents

The Modern Serial Killer 1

Before the Murders 10

College Years 21

The Murderous Monster Emerges 46

In Broad Daylight 69

The Next Move 89

The Lethal New Year 113

Monster Unmasked 129

To Tallahassee 149

Monster Caged 186

The Modern Serial Killer

Saturday, January 15, 1978, there was no heat to be found during the brisk winter evening in Tallahassee. It was known to drop down to the forties during the month. But Nita Neary didn't mind. The twenty-year-old walked beside her boyfriend after a night out. A sense of safety and security was felt on the Florida State University campus. They passed by the disco next door where music no longer played. It was where some of her sorority sisters had shared a few drinks that evening. But at 3:00 am, most of the nightlife simmered down. The last few revelries trickled home. Nita shared a goodnight kiss with her boyfriend as he brought her to the entrance of Chi Omega, her sorority and home. Nita went to punch the code for the lock in to find the door was already unlocked. This wasn't odd as many of the girls came and went, especially late night during the weekend. Though, she made sure to lock the door behind her. She moved through the house, flipping the lights the other girls left on as she passed through.

Thud.

Nita stopped. She turned around and glanced out one of the windows. She thought her boyfriend might have fallen outside, but there was nothing in the desolate parking lot underneath the heavy night sky.

But the echoes of running footsteps overhead caught her attention. They raced down the hall on the second story. Nita assumed it was one of her sorority sisters still awake, coming to see who was getting in so late. She made her way to the foyer. Her heart dropped into her stomach. This was not a sister.

The figure of a man bolted down the stairs, crouching at the front door. She could not move, could not speak. Her instincts told her to freeze. Nita watched as the man wearing a cap pulled over his eyes, reached for the doorknob with his left hand, and in his right, he clutched what she made out to be a wooden club. Before she could draw another breath, in that instant, he was gone. All she caught was his profile in the dim light.

Nita did not know it, but she had narrowly escaped death.

She locked the front door then. Her brain rattled in search of an explanation. It was not uncommon for the other girls to sneak a boy into the sorority house. Still, she wasted no time waking her roommate. Together they checked the downstairs, but nothing appeared to be amiss. But Nita could not shake the visual of the club. Why would someone need that? They woke the house president. Nita barely finished describing the scene when Karen Chandler emerged from her bedroom. She was bent forward, groggy and incoherent. The other girls first thought that she was drunk, suffering from overindulging that night, but then they saw her hands clutching her head. Blood ran down her face, matting her hair, and staining her nightgown. Almost every bone in Chandler's face had been broken by sheer force. She could do nothing more than whisper weakly for help.

In her bedroom, they found Chandler's roommate, Kathy Kleinar. Her jaw completely unhinged, blood ran from her mouth. She sat, legs crossed on the bed, rocking back and forth as gurgling sounds came from her. It sounded like she was calling out for her parents.

Panic swept over the sorority house. The girls rose, flooding the halls in a sea of chaos and fear. Who had done this? Why? Were they safe? All questions with the only answer—it was clear they had been attacked. They phoned the police, who arrived quickly onto the scene.

But Karen Chandler and Kathy Kleinar were not the only two victims, two other sorority members had been paid a visit, but they, unfortunately, did not survive the monstrous onslaught.

Their home had become a target that night. A place for a monster to sink into and claim possession. They never had a choice, and even if they had wanted to, they most likely would not have been able to stop him.

But to Nita that cold night, there was no monster crouched below her front door. It was not a beast, but an average looking man. A man she might see on any day-to-day basis. Who would have no cause to raise any red flags or alarms. At times, it was a face many would describe as handsome, even beautiful. A full-toothed smile and shining bright blue eyes. It was a face that could disarm both man and woman, encourage, and seduce.

It was the face of Theodore Robert Bundy, and he had made their home the first stop on his last binge of murders. It would end twelve days later after he raped and murdered twelve-year-old Kimberly Leach.

He was an expert at concealing the demon that lurked beneath his skin. The one that attacked the women of Chi Omega and thirsted for blood and violence. A part of him he had no choice but to feed. When exactly the killings began remains a mystery, but it was clear once Ted began nothing could stop him.

To the outside world, Ted was nothing more than a man with a bright future ahead of him. He had plans, ambitions, and goals. He was committed to a long term relationship that might have easily led to marriage and the creation of a new family. His eyes were a bright blue. His nose straight, running above an elegant mouth. A mouth with the talent to speak trust into people. And many women would refer to that face as nothing short of beautiful. No one doubted him. Even those closest to him could not believe that he was in fact a killer. Even in the early days of his trials, he amassed his own following. Young women hoping to catch his eye. His close friends and families were unable to swallow the truth. But time has a way of revealing things, and an undeniable pattern appeared.

    His charm, humor, and handsome face were part of the reason he could so easily blend into the shadows and whisk women off the street. His demeanor and appearance gave him the ability to move about the world undetected, a silent and dangerous killer. He was able to abduct and murder in broad daylight surrounded by hundreds of people. Numerous times he stalked young college-aged women, approaching them. Either luring them with a feigned act of injury or by sheer force, Ted would then bludgeon them, knocking them cold. He would take their unconscious, limp bodies hundreds of miles away to the mountains to have his way with them, dump their bodies, and strip them of their personal belongings. Sometimes, he'd make the return trip to revisit their remains and have sex with their corpses. Upon discovery, their skulls told the story of his madness and anger, and what little was left of their flesh showed the vile acts he inflicted upon them.

Many struggled to understand what exactly went wrong in Bundy's life. Someone so appealing should never have turned into such a deadly foe. How could a rising law student with a whole world of potential become the definition of the modern-day serial killer?

The truth to why will never be known. Even Ted Bundy himself admitted there was no point to which he could look back and say it was the start. "I don't think anybody doubts whether I've done some bad things. The question is: what, of course, and how and, maybe even most importantly, why?" But it is a fact. Ted Bundy was a monster. His ability to compartmentalize and rationalize freed him from the need to care. He was incapable of experiencing guilt. His guard was high. He built a mental fortress around himself, and in himself, what he described as "the entity." This entity would unleash itself and grow with more negative energy. It cannot be attributed to split personality or schizophrenia, but some believe it was just a piece of Ted. A piece he wanted and created. It was how he saw himself, broke away, and kept his two lives separate.

And like a dark, silent plague that fell across the US, Theodore Robert Bundy manifested a fear that had not previously been known.

For Ted and "the entity," the satisfaction did not come from the act of raping and mutilating beautiful women; it came from the power of possession. That was Ted's ultimate goal—to own the women he killed. It was in their death and his union with them. That is how they fell under his possession. Ted described it, "Murder is not about lust and it's not about violence. It's about possession. When you feel the last breath of life coming out of the woman, you look into her eyes. At that point, it's being God."

Before the Murders

In 1946, Eleanor "Louise" Cowell entered the Elizabeth Lund Home for Unwed Mothers in Burlington, Vermont. Twenty-two years old at the time, the young woman scared and unsure was seven months pregnant. Without the father present, she decided to spend a total of sixty-three days at the home, away from prying eyes. She was the eldest of three daughters, modest, and worked as a department store clerk.

On November 24, she could never have imagined the small baby with bright blue eyes entering the world that day would grow up to become one of America's deadliest men. She named him Theodore Robert Cowell. Ted for short. She'd always loved that name.

The true identity of Theodore's father is one cloaked in mystery. Ted's birth certificate has Lloyd Marshall, a young pilot listed in the Air Force. But later on, Louise would mention a rakish sailor by the name of Jack Worthington, who she claimed to have come from old money. After further inquiry, investigators would never find any military records of Worthington. Neither of these men has ever been confirmed or been proven to exist at all. This left the young Theodore Robert Cowell fatherless. Other rumors stemmed from darker origins. Some believe that Louise's own father raped her, fathering Ted.

But Ted did not grow up without a father figure.

Samuel Cowell, Louise's father was a violent, ill-tempered man. Known throughout the town as a raging drunk, an outspoken bigot, ranting about various minority and religious groups. He reportedly kicked the family dog and would whip around the neighborhood cats by their tails. The abuse was not exclusive to animals. It was said Samuel Cowell in a fit of anger pushed one of his daughters down the stairs because she overslept. He had been caught on several occasions, having a conversation with no one. Cowell also kept a pornography collection his young grandson viewed at will. He may have also abused his wife, who was known to suffer from agoraphobia and extreme bouts of depression. These mental illnesses were treated with electric shock therapy. Toward the end of her life, she stopped leaving her home altogether.

It was Samuel who insisted Louise bring her illegitimate son home to be raised not as Louise's son but as her brother. In a bid to hide the true nature of the baby and shame from the community, Ted spent the first three years of his life believing that his grandparents were his parents, and his mother was indeed his much older sister.

There is no hard evidence that Samuel Cowell ever abused his grandson.

According to Ted, he never suffered from the hands of his grandfather, and for the most part, idolized him. Ted romanticized his grandfather and their relationship, never speaking poorly of him. He saw Samuel Cowell as a role model. Although, it will never be known if Ted suffered any abuse at the hands of his grandfather. Surely witnessing the abuse of women at a young age shaped him and perhaps curbed Ted Bundy's young mind toward violence against women.

Ted's time under his grandfather's rule was short but no doubt impactful. In 1950, Louise packed up and moved out to Tacoma, Washington. This allegedly followed a night where Louise's sister Julie awoke suddenly to her young nephew placing knives in and around her bed. He said nothing. A dazed look in his eyes.

This stupefied transformation happened more than once. Ted morphed into another being, as though his cheerful demeanor was lost to a whole new unrecognizable person. His great aunt witnessed one such transformation while waiting with her sweet nephew at a train station. As she watched her young nephew, a sudden fear of him overtook her. He was no longer her sweet Ted. Before her was an unrecognizable person. It happened almost instantly as if darkness came over him.

Perhaps this change in behavior spurred Louise to move Ted away from the toxicity of her father. Maybe a new city would be what her troubled son needed. The reason for her move is uncertain, but she settled down with cousins out in Tacoma and pursued a fresh start. Hiding the shame of her illegitimate child sharing the same name as his Great Uncle and mother. She changed his last name from Cowell to Nelson.

As Ted later recollects, he was upset by the move. No part of him wanted to leave the comfort of his home in Philadelphia or his grandfather whom he loved. He never understood his mother's need to move.

But Louise was looking forward to her new life. She began work as a secretary at the Council of Churches' offices. She became friends with some coworkers. Eventually, one girlfriend talked her into attending an adult singles night at a local Methodist Church. It was there in the warm summer of '51, Louise met John Culpepper Bundy. John was an ex-military cook now working at the Madigan Hospital as a hospital chef. He was kind and soft-spoken, born and raised in North Carolina. Ted hated his slow southern drawl; in his mind that made Johnnie sound slow. It showcased he was unlettered. But to Louise, Johnnie Bundy wasn't complicated, and they had an immediate connection. It didn't take long for a young single mother to fall in love.

Johnnie enjoyed that Louise was a God-fearing woman. She was sweet, and he didn't question her or pry about her son. He accepted them both. That was enough for her, and so, she and Johnnie were married. Ted, upon adoption by John, was given his final last name—Bundy.

But Ted was not as accepting of his new stepfather. It was clear the cook's presence was bothersome. He would later describe planning a scene in the department store Sear's parking lot, where he wet his pants. This tantrum was most likely caused by jealousy over his mother, and that this new man would cause more disruption in Ted's life.

Within the next several years, Louise and Johnnie had four more children together. All of whom Ted spoke fondly and loved dearly.

Ted recounted his whole childhood with deep fondness. He described his life with picturesque settings and memories.

Ted spent the hot summer days outside, playing marbles or football. "First grade I was a somewhat champion frog-catcher," Bundy reminisced. "I mean, I was a frog man." He was active in Boy Scouts. And every Sunday the Bundy family made their way to church. Even his mother echoed Bundy's rose-colored memories.

But others did not. Those who grew up around Ted witnessed a different child.

Young peers describe a Ted who had a fondness for scaring the other kids in the neighborhood. He enjoyed setting up Tiger traps, small, covered holes in the ground with sharp sticks at the bottom. Ted would sit and wait for someone to fall into his trap. One poor girl did and badly hurt her leg.

There were other reports of Ted Bundy masturbating in the closets at school. The other students would catch him and dump cups of ice-cold water atop of him. Ted was known to enjoy dark pulp fiction and violent pornography, perhaps to escape the world of his peers.

But he found his release in listening to late-night talk radio. He'd listen alone and in his room. When the people would call in, he'd pretend that they called in to speak with him. In his head, he'd conjure up questions to ask them, really listen as they spoke. For Ted, part of the enjoyment was the conjuring of fantasy, an escape. The talk radio gave him the ability to eavesdrop on people talking, and it gave him what he described as comfort.

He had an obsession with possessions and material goods. He felt deprived of these things. He was jealous of his cousin John and felt complete embarrassment to be seen riding in his stepfather's modest Rambler. He blamed John Bundy and would often verbally combat him. He challenged John, describing him as dimwitted. Louise often stepped between the two, acting as the mediator.

Even more angst was seen in how Ted resented his stepfather. They were a lower-middle-class family, and Ted hated it. He took every opportunity to take a jab at John, who was quick to temper, almost as quick as Ted.

Ted continued to emotionally pull away from the family as he got older. He was known to be withdrawn with only a few close friends. The other students saw him as a bit of a loner. A speech impediment left him with a stutter, and he struggled desperately with self-confidence.

As Ted matured, the girls took note of his handsome features. Ted only had one date in high school. He claimed to not know exactly what to do with the opposite sex and at times he felt left behind. When his friends spoke about anything sexual, all of it seemed to go over his head. He described himself in an interview, "I didn't think anything was wrong, necessarily. I wasn't sure what was wrong and what was right. All I knew was that I felt a bit different." Though others would see Ted as funny, they noticed that he lacked the confidence to back it up.

Despite all this, Ted did all right with schoolwork, maintaining a B average. With a lean athletic build, he took up several sports. It was in high school he developed a love for skiing and ran track and field. The failure to be on the basketball team because he was "too small" gnawed away at Ted. The rejection was what he considered a traumatic experience.

But even with such failure, he always claimed he would become someone great. He saw himself as predestined for something bigger.

It was in his adolescence, he developed the love and obsession of spying on young women. He quickly became a peeping tom. In the evening under the cover of darkness, he would sneak away to peer into neighbors' windows. He caught glimpses of beautiful young women from behind curtains unbeknownst to them. A monster lurked in the shadows.

Ted returned to the same homes. These could be homes he found on the paper route he had when delivering the *Tacoma News Tribune* or of the lawns he cut. Either way, this voyeuristic streak grew and festered in the young Ted Bundy. He was never caught, and therefore Louise would never have any reason to suspect her son's fondness for the perverse growing. Quite the opposite. The young Ted quickly learned how to don the mask of normal for the world, learning from a young age how to hide his true monstrous nature.

His streak of criminal activities did not stop here. Ted committed petty crimes throughout his youth. He stole what he needed, coming from a family where every penny counted. Often, he stole ski equipment to use on weekend ski trips up in snowy mountain resorts. He and several others met together in a group to forge their own tickets.

But the divide in the two different Ted's was already beginning to develop. His outward demeanor he adopted in his youth had everyone fooled until years later. His closest friend could not fathom that the same young man who rushed to his back porch in late November brimming with excitement at the first fall of snow to start skiing, could be the same mass murderer who found enjoyment in stealing the lives of young women.

College Years

In 1965, Theodore Robert Bundy graduated from Wilson High School and enrolled at the University of Puget Sound that fall, where his Uncle Jack worked. He lived at home during his first year and didn't declare a major right away. Ted believed he just didn't have what he described as "the skill or social acumen to cope with it." The monotonicity of schoolwork chewed away at him, and his social life was for the most part lackluster. He maintained what few friends from high school he had, but nothing more. He found his time at Puget to be incredibly lonely, but the craving for a beautiful companion to spend time with kept him fixated.

But a drastic change would spark in Ted the following year.

Ted quickly developed the social skills and charm he became so famous for within the next year when he enrolled at the University of Washington. A skill he would harness to lure these young women to their deaths. It would take practice and effort to get it right. Like an actor preparing for a role, Bundy would rehearse conversations, plan every one of his social actions.

In 1966, Ted Bundy began to hone this charming wolf in sheep's skin. All he needed was the ideal playground to practice his new skills. He enrolled at the University of Washington in Seattle for the fall semester to study Chinese with the intention to improve the relationship between the United States and China.

Away from home, Ted could now fully immerse himself in crafting a new identity. He lost his timidness, establishing an entirely new role in society. People began to see Ted as an intense but extremely likable man with confidence and a direct way of speaking. He was seen as scholarly and witty. His bright blue eyes found theirs with unwavering eye contact. He smiled warmly and with ease. People were drawn to him. This was not the young shy Theodore Bundy from Tacoma, but a budding monster, beginning his transformation into what some would compare to the antichrist.

In pursuit of his dreams of working in politics, Ted began work as a volunteer for a local politician, Republican Nelson Rockefeller. The local campaign gave Ted a social life and a sense of accomplishment as well as a taste for a future he so desired. Greatness. During this time he was able to practice his charisma and take his first steps into the political world.

With newfound social skills and the appeal he always wanted, Ted was able to land himself the woman he dreamed of all those lonely years. Diane Edwards. Diane was strikingly beautiful with long brown hair, well dressed, and extremely poised. She stood at almost six feet tall and possessed a sense of worldliness. She came from a wealthy family in San Francisco, California. Bundy described her as "a beautiful dresser, beautiful girl. Very personable. Nice car, great parents." She was everything Ted had wanted to be, and now he was getting a taste.

They spent their time together, driving in Diane's expensive car. They searched for the perfect view through the winding roads and green forests of the mountains. They would park the car and whisper sweet nothings into one another's ear. Diane was everything Ted could have dreamed of. They enjoyed one another's company. Diane could not resist Ted's humor and charm. She might have been the first person to actually grow close to the soon-to-be murderer. Diane Edwards was the woman Ted might have actually seen himself marrying one day if it weren't for the rising sociopath that was buried within him.

But there was no denying the stark differences in their family's background. Ted's family did not have money like Diane's. As much as he tried to ignore it, the contrast in wealth bothered Ted. There were expectations and ideologies that Diane's family had for their daughter's future husband. The pressure swelled around Ted. He was unsure of himself. He wanted nothing more than to make it work, but what he described as "petty problems" began to emerge. Diane would use her money to pay for things. Ted struggled with his academic career. His grades began to spiral. Diane caught glimpses of the cracking mask Ted gracefully wore.

Ted began to change his mind about his previous intentions to improve the relationship between the United States and China. He landed a scholarship at Stanford University's Chinese Institute, but he could not sustain his grades, crumbled under the pressure, and soon left.

He returned to the University of Washington. The burn of his slight setback lingered on his shoulders. His academics were falling apart. Ted was internally fragmenting, and the consuming fear that he would lose Diane finally came true.

In 1968, Diane Edwards graduated and returned to her home state of California. The fear of losing Diane haunted Ted. He noticed her letters became less frequent as did her calls, until one day she finally called him up to inform him they were finished. She'd grown weary of his once charming boyishness. It began to feel silly, and she was looking for a serious partner.

He'd often run up and tap her shoulder to vanish. This silly behavior simply became annoying. Diane could no longer afford to wait for Ted to match her maturity.

That was the end of any stability Ted Bundy may have had on the murderous cage binding his inner demons. A dark emptiness consumed him then. He'd lost the woman of his dreams and the burning need for revenge began to rise inside of him. The break-up took its toll. The mask he'd so expertly woven together had failed him, and he could not comprehend what happened. And so the rest of 1967, Ted wrapped himself in isolation, experiencing what he considered one of his worst years.

That is when it happened.

Ted Bundy set himself on an almost six-year plan to get his revenge on Diane.

But his path of destruction didn't just stop with her.

After the breakup, Ted needed a change of scenery. He needed to get out and escape the place of memories of Diane. A fresh start for himself. He took the next semester off, informing the school he would not be returning. During this time, he flew out to be with family. He found his way to San Francisco. Then visited Denver to ski at one of the resorts. He eventually returned to his original home of Philadelphia.

It was during this time some believe Ted uncovered the truth about his father when, by chance, he came across his birth certificate. Others claim it occurred earlier in his teenage years. Perhaps, Ted was previously unaware of his illegitimacy. Perhaps this was the last blow to the fragile mental state Ted was in.

Either way, after the break-up with Diane Edward, Ted Bundy was never the same.

He may have lost the love of his life, but a new year came.

He found himself a small apartment and returned to Seattle in the spring. He also developed a friendship with a man named Richard. Ted, only twenty-one, hadn't had much experience with criminal activity aside from petty theft and counterfeit ski lift tickets. But Richard introduced him into a new world of much riskier behavior. He began stealing and shoplifting, though he never took money. For Ted, it was all about obtaining things. Things that he dreamed of owning as a child and teenager. All he had to do was simply reach out and take it.

He was never caught. An incredible feat. He dressed well and combed his hair. He wanted to present himself in a dignified but forgettable manner. He would walk into stores stealing televisions, artwork, clothing, anything Ted decided he wanted.

Not everything that happened to Ted was negative. During a random encounter with a friend on a street corner. Ted was given another opportunity to hone his social and political skills in July of 1968. And without hesitation, Ted left the job of parking cars at a fancy yacht club and immersed himself in the Republican Art Fletcher's campaign for lieutenant governor.

Here he could use his contagious smile. In this setting, Ted could sweet-talk his way into social circles far too elite for the middle-class college drop out. Ted became well-liked. He caught the eye of Fletcher and became his personal driver. Ted loved working in politics. He fully immersed himself, being a full supporter of "the establishment." He was not one to side with the hippies or the poor. Had he stayed in college, he'd be well into his junior year during this time, but Ted was learning other skills with his work. Seamlessly, he continued to work on his social acumen. He developed his mask, presented himself in the most dignified of manners, stealing the clothes he needed to be the best dressed. None of the fellow campaign members noticed any sign of Ted's inner demons developing.

After Art Fletcher lost the campaign, Ted took a temporary job in sales for a department store. Here he could steal what he wanted, but he also found he had quite the knack for sales, especially when it came to the female customers. Ted Bundy could get them to buy anything.

Once he saved up enough cash, Ted made his way back to his roots, Philadelphia. He didn't have it in him to return to

Washington, not after the fall out with Diane. Instead, he settled with enrolling at Temple University in January of 1969. He did fine with his time at Temple, excelling at his drama classes. He learned about makeup and acting, but it was during this time, Ted realized his face lacked any defining traits. The slightest adjustment like gaining weight or parting his hair differently completely changed his appearance. He decided he could be anyone and look any way he wanted. A judge would later describe Ted to have the face of "a changeling."

It was now when his thirst to harm young women grew.

He continued his habits of prowling through the night, peering through windows of beautiful coeds, watching them from the shadows. This was the time for him to refine his abilities as an abductor, a man with shining bright eyes that whisked women away to their deaths.

His habit of peeping began as a child and never stopped. Ted's twisted fantasies fueled his desires. It was only a matter of time until these fantasies compelled him to act. He indulged in pornography showcasing male violence toward women. His taste and need for violent sexual release grew like a wildfire. Viewing women from afar quickly lost its ability to satisfy. Ted needed more.

He later admitted to his first failed attempt at kidnapping in New Jersey during this time on the East Coast. He bought himself a disguise, nothing more than a wig and fake mustache. With a racing heart and nerves pumping through him, Ted approached the woman with the attempt to strike up a conversation, but it was to no avail. He failed, and she escaped.

The soon-to-be killer became painfully aware of how much preparation the task demanded. The desire and anger were there, but Ted was an amateur. Unsure. He had no plan for the execution. Unfortunately, he found a way to teach himself with trial and error. Though his first documented attack was not until 1974, Ted alluded to Dr. Art Norman in an interview days before his death sentence that he murdered two women while living in Philadelphia. Perhaps in these two murders, Ted learned a few lessons. He found the streets of Philly overly crowded and dirty. He may have found there were too many eyes readily available to catch him sleuthing through the shadows of homes. Dumping a body with many witnesses around would have proven a lofty challenge.

Theodore Bundy left the state of Pennsylvania. He moved back home to Washington. Here there were ample forests and trails hidden away. All of which, he knew well. He rented his own apartment in Seattle and lived for the most part quietly, his head down. He earned money through odd jobs including the physically taxing work at a lumber mill. His landlords Ernest and Frieda Rogers were pleased with their kind and helpful tenant.

They found him to be extremely polite and tidy. He was eager to help with errands and around the house, often running to the store for them. Frieda recalled the time, she and Ted were having coffee in her kitchen when a fly made an unwanted appearance. Frieda naturally began to swat at the buzzing nuisance, but Ted leaped from his seat. He didn't want her to kill the fly. "Don't kill it!" he shouted, choosing to coax the bug out the window instead. In the Rogers' minds, their tenant wouldn't even hurt a fly.

He had thoughts of what to do with his future, possibly finish his degree. But he was not quite ready to return to the University of Washington. Still, without any direct plan, the rising beast inside festered. And then, Ted had what he might consider a stroke of luck. He lived just around the corner from a tavern frequented by many of the college students. He would go every once in a while, have a few drinks, and take his shot of bringing home a woman.

On September 30, 1969, Ted Bundy entered the smoky, rock 'n' roll filled Sandpiper Tavern. His plan for the night consisted of nothing more than to sip on a few cold beers alone, but then his eyes fell upon a lovely woman. One woman, he would enter a six-year relationship with, but it would never be normal.

He approached her first, making his way across the bar. He asked her to dance and at first, she declined. "I'm sorry," Liz said coolly, "I don't dance." But her attention never left the well-dressed, ruggedly handsome man. As the night progressed, twenty-four-year-old Elizabeth Kloepfer made her move. He had moved on to dancing with one of Liz's friends, and she took note. She approached Ted at his table, who was slightly taken aback by her forwardness. There was an immediate connection. The conversation flowed through the night. Ted learned about the recently divorced mother of one who worked as a secretary for Washington University's medical department. He weaved a story about finishing up at Temple University with plans to enroll in law school shortly. He also mentioned he was writing a book on the Vietnam war. She didn't believe the part about the book so much, but either way, it didn't take much for Liz to fall for the smooth-talking murderer. Elizabeth described their first encounter. "The chemistry between us was incredible," she wrote in her book *The Phantom Prince: My Life with Ted Bundy*.

"I was already planning the wedding and naming the kids. He was telling me that he missed having a kitchen because he loved to cook. Perfect. My prince."

Together they continued the night out after the bar. Ted went with Liz to pick up her young daughter from the babysitter's, and as they drove through the cool Seattle night, Ted held the two-year-old Tina in his lap. They chatted away with easy conversation. It was effortless. Ted gently carried a sleeping Tina to Liz's place, who invited him to stay the night. Ted was far too drunk to go home on his own.

Liz could never have known the man she brought inside her home was a monster. She was alone with only her small child. The daughter of a successful doctor from Utah, Liz's first marriage had ended quickly and painfully. She found it difficult to trust men. That was until Ted.

The two of them continued the night, though nothing sexual happened between them. Liz Kloepfer unknowingly slept beside a person who would become the most hunted man in all of America. Who knew what coursed through his mind as he laid beside a woman he'd just met. If any dark thoughts bounded through him in the stillness of her home.

Liz luckily did not share the same fate as women who left the night alone under Bundy's eye. Instead, six years would pass only to end with her battling the idea that the man she once wanted to marry was a serial killer. He left her completely dazzled, and she would rationalize away the lies he told her. His anger she would combat with her kindness. She learned how to deal with Ted and quickly became another addition to someone under his spell.

The sun rose when the next morning came. Bundy was found cooking breakfast for Liz and Tina. The relationship, after all, started in a whirlwind of happiness. Perhaps at this moment, Ted still clung to the hope and dreams of a normal life with a family of his own. With Liz now, there was a chance at that. When he left that morning, he couldn't get her out of his mind. Bundy later revealed to Stephen G. Michaud during an interview, "I loved her so much it was destabilizing. I felt such a strong love for her, but we didn't have a lot of interests in common like politics or something, I don't think we had in common." Happily, he took on the role of a doting boyfriend, doing dishes, taking out the trash. He got along well with Tina and was delighted by her.

In less than a year, the talk of marriage began to arise. Liz wanted to marry Ted. It made sense. Her parents adored him; they shared a group of friends. They lived together, basically, as any normal married couple would. She was unsettled with their lifestyle and wanted to take the next step with Bundy. Ted finally agreed to the marriage, and after one trip to the courthouse, a fight ended with the certificate being ripped up by Bundy. He told her it was too soon for marriage, but in truth, he could no longer keep up the charade of the lies he told. When she found that two years were left between him and receiving his undergraduate, she was upset. But Ted had a way of working his charm on Liz. She believed in her confident, smart man. So she propped him up. She gave him a few hundred bucks for tuition, urging him to finish. If her future husband became a lawyer then together they would have a suitable life. With Ted, Liz believed she'd hit the jackpot.

Ted wasted no time. He was ready to get back to the University of Washington. In the spring of 1970, he finally enrolled for the last time. He majored in psychology and performed well in school. He later admitted his choice in psychology was spurred on by his need to understand himself. He dove into his studies, never missing an exam question and writing a praised paper on schizophrenia. Many of his professors enjoyed him as a student. Perhaps it was the support of his girlfriend that aided in this newfound confidence. Ted no longer floundered with schoolwork. He'd found a purpose again and it fueled him. He also worked as a delivery driver for Ped Line Medical Supplies. But he hadn't quite stopped his ways of sneaking around and thieving. He would steal from the medical supplies company's tools to later use on his murderous rampages.

To the outside world, Theodore Bundy was a man well on his way to success. He continued work in Washington's Republican Party's scene and helped Dan Evans run. He'd perfected his social expertise, and now he had a budding career full of possibilities. Ivy League schools were in his scope, and he applied to several for law school.

Ironically enough, during this time, Ted worked at the Seattle Crisis Clinic saving lives as a telephone counselor. Coworkers took note of how well he handled the tough calls and managed to prevent several suicides. Ted found he had the best connections with lonely, abandoned women, those whose husbands or mates abused them. Once a week he would stay on the phone with the frantic and distressed until he heard the police entering the caller's home.

Everything seemed to be working out well until the summer of 1972. Ted began to experience bouts of depression and an increased need for release of his darkest fantasies. One of Liz's closest friends caught Ted late in the night wandering around in the yard. She assumed, based on past experiences he was committing an act of thievery, but the truth was far more sinister. Ted was sneaking through the night, continuing to feed his ever-growing appetite for inhuman fantasies.

Ted received a long line of rejections from various law schools denying admittance based on his less-than-impressive Law School Aptitude score. The dream of furthering his career seemed to be at a standstill. Luckily, with a letter of recommendation from Governor Dan Evans, Ted received the news that he was finally accepted into the University of Utah's law school. He would wait about a year before he began school again.

After the November 1972 election, Ted switched gears from politics to working at Seattle Crime Commission for a month. This gave him insight into how the police worked. He analyzed statistics on white-collar crime and even wrote reports on young women who were sexually assaulted. With some help from his political ties, Ted began to work at the King County Office of Law and Justice Planning. It was his noted interest to learn how attacks were committed and how the police handled these reports. This window gave him the time to devour as many reports and statistics as he possibly could. It was his own personal library, teaching him how to commit the perfect crime.

Ted was on the rise again. His life was moving forward.

Listening to the advice from a friend, Ted decided to remain in Washington to begin law school at the University of Puget Sound. He was persuaded to not go out of state in Utah. Attending the new school would put Ted in the position to meet local lawyers and set him up for more success in politics. Ted saw the advantages and enrolled at the University of Puget Sound's nightly law school. Instead of being honest with the University of Utah, Ted crafted a story to explain why he could no longer attend their law program. He informed them it had to do with an automobile accident.

With the promise of law school on the horizon, no one would have guessed this rising star with so much promise had evil brewing within him. The income was good. He had a steady woman in his life. Ted was brimming with confidence. This new Bundy even caught the eye of his old flame Diane Edwards. Though Ted claimed to only love Liz, he'd never forgotten Diane Edwards. On a business trip to California, Ted reconnected with his first girlfriend. She was completely swept away by this new persona. In her eyes, this new Bundy was in control. The man she'd always dreamed of.

Diane's returning interest in Bundy was exactly what he hoped for. Now, he could enact his revenge. The two began seeing one another, all while Ted continued on with his sweet Liz. For months, he spent quiet nights with Liz and Tina, all while taking Diane to expensive ski resorts and restaurants. All of this was part of Ted Bundy's ability to live two incredibly separate lives. This was Ted's specialty. His uncanny ability to shift between morals would later allow him to go from raping and murdering women to returning home to his loved ones without skipping a beat or step. It is what psychologists call compartmentalization. In Ted's mind, he could easily separate different selves from each other, so they never touched nor crossed.

Toward the end of summer in 1973, Ted drove over to meet his good friend Ross Davis. Ross stood in the driveway, while Ted rummaged through the back of his recently purchased '68 Volkswagen Beetle. Ted was known to pack a lot in his car. So it wasn't odd for the trunk to be full, Ross caught something unusual among the clutter. Handcuffs. Nothing came from it, but it was odd enough for Ross to remember years down the road.

The school year came, and Ted began law school, only to prove a complete failure. He kept this hidden from Liz and Diane Edwards. His arrival at Puget Sound's law school left him with a bitter taste in his mouth. It lacked everything he had dreamed about. He held a large amount of disdain for what he considered a second rate law school and he quickly fell to the bottom of the program. His goals were indeed escaping him. The mounting pressure rose through him, twisting with rage.

In December, he decided to secretly reapply a second time to the law program at the University of Utah. He was accepted in but wouldn't leave until the fall of 1974.

He had a slight second wind with his studies after the acceptance and tried a bit more with his remaining time at Puget Sound. He'd spend a lot of his time in the law library studying. But he entered cycles of depression. He struggled with the wish to succeed and the reality of his mounting failures. He'd wear his mask around others, having them believe he was still on the road to triumph.

The holidays came and Liz headed home to Utah, but Ted stayed in Seattle to be joined with Diane Edwards. For a week they stayed in a friend's apartment. The whole summer and fall, Ted had kept up the charade of a changed man, and Diane was completely sold. They spoke of marriage for several days, and finally, he proposed. Diane said yes and returned to California with the notion she was engaged to the man of her dreams. He kissed her at the airport before she left, only to drive home to Liz, where he'd share a nice warm dinner and a bed that night.

Ted never went out of his way to speak with Diane again. He had conned her. It was all part of his revenge. She would call him in February of 1974 after Ted was well into his murderous rampage. She demanded to know why, but Ted gave no explanation. He did not apologize. She hung up telling him to never contact her again. She hung up the phone, but Ted was unphased. He continued drinking his beer, relieved to put Diane behind him.

And in those cold, bitter first months of 1974, the sociopath had already taken on its final transformation, and Ted Bundy would become one of America's most famous serial killers.

The Murderous Monster Emerges

January 4, 1974, twenty-one-year-old Karen Sparks finished watching television in her living room. She turned off the screen, making her way down to her basement bedroom. Like most college students at the University of Washington, she shared a house with three roommates. She was a dancer with a kind face and lovely, long brunette hair. She crawled into bed. Being in the basement, Karen Sparks was completely separated from her other roommates. She most likely didn't mind this, since they were all men.

Minutes before, Theodore "Ted" Bundy traveled in the cold winter night toward a house that was only a short walk from his apartment. He had made this stroll several times before. He knew the route well, and he'd have seen the house enough to know exactly who was peacefully asleep in the basement bedroom. A northside window gave a perfect view into Spark's room for anyone who might have lurked by, searching.

At some point deep in the darkest hours of the cold winter night, Ted Bundy made his way silently into Karen's bedroom. Crowbar gripped tightly in hand. In the shadows of the room, there he found Karen fast asleep. Her dark hair laid atop the pillow as each of her shallow breaths rose and fell.

Ted Bundy's arm rose. The crowbar fell against Karen's head and bludgeoned her skull. There was no stopping him now. Karen's blood splattered everywhere. It ran along her bedding and splattered on the walls painting a gory picture. She did not have time to cry out for help. In his maniacal fever, Ted ripped a metal rod from her bed frame and sexually assaulted her with a speculum. When his thirst was satiated, Ted slipped out of her room and back into the world.

It wasn't until 2:30 pm that one of Karen's roommates decided to check on their roommate. The student assumed Karen chose to lazily sleep the day away. Out of politeness, they cracked the door open slowly so as to not disturb her slumber, but what they found was a sight straight out of a horror movie.

There was Karen, or rather, what was left of her. Her head and body had been savagely beaten. Blood was everywhere. Ted must have left under the assumption he had killed Karen, but he was wrong. She miraculously survived, suffering permanent brain damage and remained in a coma for ten days after her attack.

Theodore Bundy would not make that mistake again.

Over the course of his total rampage, Ted Bundy would be responsible for thirty-six women's deaths, but some experts believe his tally could potentially be near 100. The extent of his killing will never be fully known.

But the first documented murder at the hands of Ted Bundy was a twenty-one-year-old named Lynda Ann Healey. She was another student at the University of Washington who lived only minutes from Karen Sparks.

January 31, 1974, Lynda Ann Healey was a senior who began her scholarly career considering a music degree but ended up majoring in psychology. After graduation, she planned to help students with cognitive deficiencies. Outside of school, Lynda could be heard on the radio hosting a popular show that many of the Seattle students listened to. She was a ski reporter for Northwest Ski Promotions. Getting up early to share news to the local snow bunnies and announce the weather for the slopes. Ted, an avid skier, may have tuned in to hear Lynda during those mornings. Perhaps it was the reason why Bundy singled her out as a potential target.

Lynda was popular, she had a close group of friends that she often drank with at a local spot, Dante's. A few months prior, Lynda and three of her friends, recently moved out of the dorms and into a rental home at 5517 12th Street N.E. Like Karen Sparks, Lynda always slept in the basement. The difference between the two was Linda had a roommate close within earshot. Her space was divided by nothing more than a thin piece of plywood. On the other side was one of her roommates, Karen Skaviem. Sound easily traveled between the two makeshift bedrooms. But college students are not so bothered by the lack of privacy.

That evening, Lynda cooked a casserole for her friends. Around this time, Ted was attending his night classes at Puget Sound. Lynda and her friends had plans to go grab a few pitchers of beer at Dante's, near Seattle's University District. The group of friends kept to themselves mostly during the night. They enjoyed the college catered atmosphere, sipping on the cold drinks, laughing, and talking. Lynda was in a great mood that evening. She had been feeling a bit under the weather the few days prior but that had cleared up on its own.

Around 9:30 pm, the group of friends made their way back to their home. No one noticed a lingering shadow of a man trailing behind. Nothing felt out of place. Of course, none of them would ever have reason to suspect there was. Once inside, they gathered in the living room to relax and watch a couple of shows. Lynda slipped off to her bedroom to make a call to her boyfriend. She spoke with him for an hour. Then hung out with one of her other girlfriends. It was a typical night for any college student, and Lynda was in great spirits. She was excited that her parents and boyfriend were coming over for dinner the following day. There was no sign that Lynda ever planned to take off the next day. Quite the opposite, she had reasons to stay. Lynda eventually retired to her room for the night.

Perhaps it was nothing, or perhaps it was the foreshadowing of the deadly predator waiting outside to attack his selected prey. But one roommate noticed a shadow pass by the window.

At some point in the night, Ted Bundy emerged from the dark night and slipped into the dwelling of the four young women. He made his way silently through the home and into Lynda's bedroom, where he found her fast asleep. He did not dare waste a second. With a crowbar pressed tightly into his hand, he struck Lynda's head. Ted would not make the same mistake he had with Karen Sparks. He abducted Lynda after he removed her bloodstained nightgown and dressed her in a fresh pair of jeans and a clean shirt.

Where he took her unconscious body next is unclear, but he raped then murdered Lynda Ann Healey, dumping her body thirty miles east of Seattle on the side of Taylor mountain.

It was in the early hours of the morning, 5:30 am, when Karen Skaviem, Lynda's housemate who shared the basement wall, woke up to the sound of Lynda's radio-alarm. She assumed her friend had woken up and was listening to the radio. But thirty minutes later, Karen noticed that Lynda's alarm was still going. At 6:30 am, one hour after Lynda's alarm had gone off, the phone rang. The Northwest Ski Promotions called. They wanted to know why Lynda hadn't shown up for her shift. This was extremely uncharacteristic of Lynda. Karen, slightly worried, went inside Lynda's room. She called out for her friend, then flipped on the light switch.

Lynda Ann Healey was gone. The radio still played hauntingly in the empty space. It was immediately noticed, the bed was in fact perfectly made. There were no wrinkles in the sheets. This was uncharacteristic as Lynda never made her bed, especially in the early hours of the morning when she scrambled to make it to work on time. None of the other roommates had any idea where Lynda would have been. She wouldn't have just disappeared, especially without calling into work.

Perhaps she was with her boyfriend or gone to see her family. None of these rooted in anything other than an idea, and the unease transformed into panicked fear. The fact remained. No one knew where Lynda was. Her friends and family could only guess.

Officers arrived at the scene and began their investigation. It was not completely unheard of for a young woman to disappear, especially at this age. The first report was nothing too unusual. They took notes on the friends' activity from the night before. They noticed Lynda's missing clothes, but she could have just packed them before she left. When the report was finished, the two officers drove off.

It was at 8:00 pm that night. The phone rang once again. When it was answered, the hello was met with nothing more than silence. Quickly they redialed, but the voice on the other line refused to speak. All that was heard were a faint few breaths on the other side. This would happen twice more throughout the night. A mysterious call with nothing to say but complete silence.

Before midnight, a homicide detective arrived at the home. He immediately entered Lynda's room. He pulled back the bed to find red bloodstains on the sheets and pillows, as well as her nightgown hanging in the closet, with red blood dried around the back of the neck. The police had decided to write off as nothing more than a nosebleed.

But Lynda never returned, never called again. When the comparison was made between her attack and that of Karen Sparks, fear began to spread. Someone out in the world was bold enough to walk into a home, brutally rape, and beat these women undetected like a nightmarish phantom shrouded in the darkness.

Days became weeks and then months. Washington state would soon learn the gravity of this horror.

Nineteen years old, Donna Mason attended Evergreen State College and was known as a free spirit. She was known to hitchhike, a common practice at the time, enjoy concerts, and hanging out with friends. She wrote poems and was interested in the occult. She would head out at times without telling anyone, stay out all night, and was known to partake in some illicit drugs. It was what the detectives would later classify as "high risk." A few months before her disappearance, Donna had hitchhiked to Oregon without telling anyone.

On March 12, 1974, Donna Mason got ready for a jazz concert she planned to attend with her friends. She slipped on a warm, fuzzy coat to help fend off the springtime chill. There was a slight drizzle of rain common to the west side of the states. As she headed out, there was no reason to fear the paths she had taken so many times before. This was a familiar route she knew well, and someone like Donna rarely got scared at such a trivial task.

At some point between Donna Mason's home and the concert, she was taken. Disappeared into the cold, rainy night. Whether she was enticed by the charm of her abductor or violently bludgeoned unconscious to be whisked away, no one will ever know. No one except Ted Bundy. Later, he would confess to decapitating her and cremating her head in his fireplace. Donna's remains were never located.

Now Ted had unleashed the killer fully. It was a part of him that would become all-consuming. Before he had been able to manage the predator desires. Under the watchful eye of his girlfriend Liz and preoccupied with his rising career, he had no room to divulge in his satanic desires. Now, nothing could stop the monster who escaped from his tormented mind. He had not gone to school on March 12, and his attendance would start to waver and drift well into April. During this month he confessed to Liz he was not doing as well as he had hoped in school. He laid on her lap as she held him, offering comfort. He told her he could not concentrate. She assumed it was the stress of law school. Little did she know his mind was consumed with thoughts of beating, raping, and murdering young women.

A pattern began to emerge within Bundy. Every month this entity inside of him needed to be fed, needed a fresh kill. Detectives quickly pinned down the timeline, but that was little help. Only after successfully murdering, would Ted be able to regain his composure for a moment, relapse back into what one might consider normalcy.

Wednesday, April 17th came, and Ted itched for another strike. Kathleen Clara D'Olivo was finishing up her studying at Boullion Library at Central Washington State Campus. She matched Ted's type, long dark hair, parted down the middle, beautiful. She caught his eye.

It was a nice spring night as she made her way outside. Kathleen gathered her books and began to return home to have her weekly call with her fiancé. To Kathleen D'Olivo, it was a normal evening. She was on her way down the sidewalk to the parking lot where her car waited, but a strange sound stopped her in her tracks.

A thud from behind her.

"I turned around, and there was a man dropping books. He was squatting, trying to pick up the books and packages," Kathleen told police. His arm was resting in a sling and metal hand brace on the other. Kathleen didn't know it at the time, but she observed Ted Bundy in a full out farce. Ted bent over putting on a show, pretending to struggle to pick up his dropped items. Nothing was abnormal about him. He was hurt after all, and Kathleen offered to help. To the common observer, one would think he was on his way to the library.

But Ted had other plans. Instead of heading to the library, Ted headed in a different direction. Kathleen immediately asked where he was going. He was kind and non-threateningly informed her, "Oh, my car is just parked right over here."

Kathleen became wary. She watched the way he moved, making sure to never let this injured man slip behind her. Something wasn't adding up in her mind. She saw his car as they walked. It was parked away from the others in a dimly lit, isolated area. Ted feigned pain, telling her how he hurt himself in a skiing accident recently. It all came naturally to him, but when they reached the car, Ted began to struggle to put the key in the door. Kathleen slid the bag from her shoulder and set it on the ground. She'd had enough. She wanted to help this man, and yet something was not sitting right with her.

Bundy dropped the key. It slipped from his fingers and fell onto the pavement. He tried to find it, but he insisted he needed help. He asked her to find it for him, but Kathleen knew better than to put herself in such a vulnerable position.

Instead, she suggested they step back and see if the metal keys would shine in the light. Luckily, she caught a glimpse of the shining metal, hurriedly plucked them from the ground, and dropped them in Bundy's hand. He said thank you, and she quickly made her exit.

Kathleen survived an encounter with a killer.

Jane Curtis would also have a dance with death after leaving the Boullion Library on a Sunday that April. Which Sunday exactly, she was not sure. In a similar fashion to Kathleen, Ted Bundy staged his act. As Jane exited the library, a man with an arm in a cast fumbled with his possessions, dropping his books, and was in need of help. She obliged to help bring his books to his car. The two walked together, deeper into isolation until they came to his brown Beetle.

Jane caught a glimpse of the sinister evil, lurking beneath Bundy's eyes. Perhaps it was a glimpse of the devil waiting to entrap her. Bundy was beginning to crack beneath his mask. He told her "Open it up," pushing his keys at her. Jane, taken aback by his forwardness, said no. Bundy grew frustrated. He couldn't wait to continue with the kill, so he unlocked the car himself and yelled "Get in!" Jane was shocked by his tone. Bundy, realizing his slip, attempted to quell the situation, but it was too late. Jane knew she was no longer helping a man in need. The books she held for Bundy fell from her hands, and Jane ran, escaping.

This would be the tactic seen over and over the following few months. Bundy would wait, his arm in a cast or sling. He would feign the need for help by dropping his books or keys. It was easy to prey on young, kind women, who saw no threat in the hurt but handsome man.

Susan Rancourt, unfortunately, did not escape. Ted Bundy enraptured her utilizing these tactics, but her disappearance was not merely dismissed as a wanderlust young woman. The same night Kathleen D'Olivo was heading to the library, Susan had started a load of laundry at the dorm's laundry room. She then decided to attend a meeting for future dorm counselors. This meeting wrapped up at 10:00 pm. Fifteen minutes later, another student caught a glimpse of a man wearing a green ski parka; the student described the man as though he walked in a daze, and with him was a young white woman wearing a yellow coat. Susan wore a yellow coat that night to the meeting. This man and the young woman were undoubtedly Ted Bundy luring Susan away through the night. Within hours of each other, Kathleen D'Olivo and Susan walked the same path, joined by the same company, on the same night.

But Susan never made it home. She was not one of the lucky ones to escape the devil. Susan Rancourt disappeared without a trace. The day Susan Rancourt disappeared, a VW resembling Ted's was spotted parked at Taylor Mountain, which was later discovered as a dumping ground for Ted.

Detectives were taking notice now. Women with long dark hair, parted in the middle were being swept away without a trace. The lack of evidence was infuriating. For all they knew, this was a monster simply kidnapping strangers. The detectives could not pinpoint a motive or the method.

Both Roberta Kathleen Parks and Brenda Ball seemingly vanished that May of 1974 in the same fashion. They disappeared without a trace. To someone like Ted Bundy, these young women were easy pickings. His work was so clean and efficient, no one could uncover evidence of their whereabouts.

May 6, the last day Brenda Ball was seen, Ted Bundy's girlfriend, Liz, invited her parents to come to town. Liz's daughter was to be baptized the next morning. That evening, the family celebrated the occasion with pizza. Ted spent his early evening with Liz and her daughter Tina, but Liz noticed Ted was acting anxious. She sensed he was off, and the fear that he might be cheating began to creep through her. It only reinforced her fears when Ted did not show up for Tina's baptism the following morning.

She began to notice a change in her sweet Ted during the spring of 1974. During this time, Ted dived deeper into his two different lives. By day he could be out playing racquetball at the courts with friends, and by night a murderous villain, raping young coeds. Liz noted Ted slipping out at night; she'd wake up in the morning to find him missing. His sudden departures became more and more frequent.

The young women continued to disappear igniting a fire of fear across Washington. The police struggled to gather what little information they could. Young women were told to travel in groups and no longer do dangerous activities such as hitchhiking. It was impossible to tell who the next target would be and how the abductor would strike. The police called it strange disappearances, but they all knew these women were never coming home.

Georgann Hawkins would have heard the rumors of the kidnapper in Washington. She was from a town near Tacoma and was in her freshman year at the University of Washington. Only eighteen years old, college life was new and exciting for her. It came easily. She was pretty and popular, known for making friends easily. A social butterfly. She was even a part of the Kappa Alpha Theta sorority; she, like Lynda Ann Healey, also lived in the U District.

She was almost finished with her spring semester. Her thoughts fell on the upcoming Spanish test. Similar to the average college student, she worried about getting good grades. Georgann only had to push through the last few school requirements, and she would be able to return home on June 13th. It was only three days away.

The night Georgann vanished, she was out with friends at a frat party. Georgann's evening began innocently. She needed a break from all the studying and was eager to have a few beers at an end-of-term party. When she finished, she and her friend left the party a little after midnight, but Georgann wanted to stop to see her boyfriend quickly. She and her friend walked to Georgann's boyfriend's, where she hung out with him for a mere thirty minutes. His house was only 100 yards from her own.

After a kiss goodbye, Georgann left the house. The back door slammed as she slipped out, alerting Duane Covey, a roommate of her boyfriend, who was in his bedroom. He popped his head out to catch Georgann leaving. They spoke briefly about the test. Covey noted during this time, down the alley, they both heard a laugh several times. This laughter could have easily been Ted Bundy, enjoying his night hunt. Giddy with delight knowing what hell he was about to unleash. She was the exact type that Ted Bundy loved. He scoured the alleyways excited to find that there was an abundance of young women to choose from. He lingered. However many minutes it took, he didn't care. He lived for the hunt.

Georgann and Covey chatted for not more than five minutes when Georgann decided it was time to retire for the night. Her final exam was the next day. Covey watched Georgann walk away until her slim form disappeared in the night. She only had 300 feet to go before she was at the doorstep of her sorority, and so, he went back to bed.

But if Covey had turned around and waited just a bit longer, he would have seen Georgann emerge from the dark with a handsome, brown-haired man limping on crutches, his leg in a cast. In her hand would be a briefcase. She and this man would, in fact, pass right underneath Covey's window and straight to her death.

How exactly Ted got Georgann to his car will forever remain a mystery, but she was clearly willing to help the pretender. At some point, whether it was when she tried unlocking the car for him or setting his briefcase down, Ted reached for his crowbar he kept beneath his car and struck quickly with precision. Georgann never had a chance. He fastened metal handcuffs around her wrists. She was gone.

The campus housemother heard a woman's scream in the late hours of the night that June 11th. She awoke and thought it was nothing more than a prank and returned to sleep.

Ted sped away from the University, an unconscious Georgann beside him in his car. The poor, young victim stirred awake several times. "And she thought she had a Spanish test the next day, and she thought I had taken her to help tutor me for a Spanish test. It was kind of odd. An odd thing to say," Bundy described. He knocked her out once more and drove until he came to a grassy rural area outside of Issaquah. It was a spot he'd most likely planned and pre-selected.

Poor Georgann did not live much longer at the desolate location under the black night sky. When she regained consciousness, Ted strangled her to death with an old piece of rope. He would continue to have his way, raping her corpse long after she drew her last breath. Ted decapitated her head, burying it twenty-five to fifty yards away from the rest of her body. He admitted to returning to her burial site. When the detective asked if it was to commit sexual acts with the body, Ted refused to answer. Georgann Hawkins' body remains lost to this very day.

Fear was mounting in the state of Washington as detectives scrambled to piece together what they knew. But this killer seemed to only be crafting a web of fear. Six women had vanished without a trace and another brutally attacked in the night. Never had there been such horror inflicted. A pattern was clear; although, the detectives would not see it on until much later. All the women Ted Bundy attacked bore a striking resemblance to his first sweetheart, Diane Edwards.

In Broad Daylight

During all of this, Ted continued to uphold the image of a family man he worked hard to build. The part of him hanging onto the American dream didn't die, but between killings, there were times when the curtain was peeled away, and the truth of his nature seeped out. Now that the killer was loose, he no longer had quite the tight leash. And there were times, friends and family witnessed his horrific form.

He informed Liz back in April of his plans to attend law school out in Utah. He cried, failing to mention he'd made the plans to move months prior to his official announcement. He also needed to secure a summer job and landed one out in Olympia at the Washington State Department of Emergency Services. Here, he worked with the search and rescue teams. The DES even worked on finding Lynda Ann Healey, Susan Rancourt, and Donna Mason. Ted began in May and caused a bit of a fluster among the female employees. They were drawn to him, and the male coworkers could not deny his natural charisma.

It was during this time he met Carol Ann Boon, a strong-willed woman. She had recently divorced her second husband and was busy raising her son. She was drawn to Ted right away, and in the beginning, their relationship was more of an affectionate friendship than anything romantic. At times, Carol would overhear Ted on the phone with Liz. There were heated conversations, and when they would end, Carol noticed Ted would be in a foul mood.

As the summer continued on, Liz grew nervous. She was after a firm commitment from Ted. She couldn't bear the idea of him taking off to Utah for a school year. She'd witnessed a few mannerisms of the monster. The fall before, she'd uncovered a bag of women's clothing. Then she found crutches as well as plaster for a cast. It was strange. His sexual appetite grew. He desired anal sex, which she refused. Liz did allow him to tie her up several times, but that act felt unnatural for her. During a discussion about his knack for thievery, Ted grew violently aggressive, threatening her, "If you ever tell anyone about this, I'll break your fucking neck." But he hadn't hurt her yet, and she believed he never would. It was not too long before Liz could no longer excuse his actions. There were moments she could not simply write off.

On July 6th, Ted and Liz planned a rafting trip down the Yakima River. It was a popular, beautiful stretch, running about fifteen miles downstream and took about five to six hours. It was sunny, a perfect summer day. They shared a few beers, talked with one another. Ted had the ability to ease Liz's worries with his smooth-talking and warm demeanor.

Then something happened.

As they progressed further down the river, Ted's mood began to shift. He began to talk less and less. This was nothing out of the ordinary. Liz didn't mind sitting beside him, enjoying the natural view of the forest around them. Suddenly, ice-cold water swirled around her. Ted without a word had lunged for

Liz, shoving her off the raft and straight into the river. Naturally, she was upset. She couldn't believe it. She shouted at Ted. He did not grin or laugh in a playful manner, nor express his sincere apology. Ted was completely unfazed by it all. He stared at her as if she might be a stranger. There was no recognition in his cold, blue eyes matching the cold water around Liz.

Perhaps for Bundy, the monster stirred, bursting at the seams. For the next day would be what many assumed his practice-run at Lake Sammamish. He would abduct two women in broad daylight. The anticipation for it all might have caused him to snap, lashing out in a violent way. A week passed and Liz, never really questioning the man she shared the past five years with, would think everything had gone back to normal.

The day before the disappearance at Lake Sammamish Park, she telephoned Ted with hopes the two of them could get together. Bundy denied her, told her he had plans. When she pressed him asking what he could possibly have going on, he simply remarked "Just things, Liz."

But that Sunday, July 14, 1974, Ted suddenly arrived at Liz's home as she readied herself to attend church. He wanted to know if she had anything on her schedule. He was anxious to know where she planned to go. She mentioned a small park, hoping his arrival meant they would in fact spend the day together.

It didn't.

It meant Ted was in the clear to commit two murders surrounded by hundreds of people. He left Liz at her doorstep, but he would call to make plans for dinner that evening, about one hour before Denise Naslund vanished from Lake Sam.

It's estimated that 40,000 people came to Lake Sammamish State Park that day. It was a warm Sunday to get out and relax, and that was exactly what everyone did twelve miles east of Seattle. There was no end to the activities being held. It ranged from the Seattle police picnic to young families watching their toddlers splash in the water. Beer kegs were set up, and a multitude of outdoor sports games abounded. Music drifted around the park as well as the smell of barbecue grilling. It was what many might consider a perfect Sunday in July.

Twenty-three-year-old Janice Ott had every intention of enjoying the park as well. She'd spent the earlier part of her morning, running errands and going to the laundromat. Probably eager to lay out. She arrived home and changed into her black bikini underneath a pair of cut off shorts and tied white shirt. According to her husband, James Ott, Janice was an organized person. She was never late. True to her described nature, she left a note for her roommate informing them that she had plans to go to Lake and catch some sun. She did not say when she would return and unfortunately she never would. Janice hopped onto her yellow ten-speed bike, knapsack on her back, and made her way to mingle with other Washington natives.

One of those natives was Janice Graham, twenty-two years old. Graham had come to Lake Sam, to spend the day out with her parents and boyfriend, whom she was waiting for near the bandstand. It was then that a young man, whom she would later guess was in his mid-twenties, with sandy blond hair, a white t-shirt with red trim at the neck, jeans and oddly enough an injured arm resting in a sling approached her. He was friendly and struck up a conversation about his friends with ease. He was waiting for friends to help unload his sailboat and gestured to his arm. He explained it was injured during a bit of racquetball. With no friends in sight, a hurt arm, and a sailboat that needed unpacking he inquired if Graham could be of assistance. She agreed. There was no reason not to. He was handsome, well dressed, and hurt after all. Together they made their way through the crowds to a brownish metallic Volkswagen Beetle. He was cheerful, keeping the conversation going.

Janice Graham had no reason to suspect anything until she noticed there was no sail atop his car nor boat on a trailer. When she asked about this, he brushed it off. "It's at my folk's house, just up the hill," he casually responded. But Graham made her exit then. She had to meet her husband and parents.

The man cheerfully thanked her as she turned around to return to her spot.

Ten minutes later, Graham would see the strange fellow again, this time walking beside a young woman, pushing a yellow ten-speed.

Janice Ott found a good spot for herself close to the water's edge. She undressed down to her black bikini and pulled her a jar of cocoa butter and some books from her knapsack, tossing them on the towel. Her green eyes sparkled in the sun and the reddish blonde hair fell around her shoulders. It wouldn't take much for the beautiful young woman to catch the prying eyes of Ted Bundy.

She hardly was there for a few moments when Ted approached her with a kind greeting. "Could you help me put my sailboat onto my car? I can't do it myself because I broke my arm." Janice eyed him for a moment. She smiled then. Being a "liberated" woman in a more open marriage, Janice Ott was hardly put off by the man and gestured for him to join her. She patted an open spot on her white towel. "Well, sit down and let's talk about it. Where's the boat?"

Carefully Ted lowered himself, he could not give up the farce of his injured arm. He sat crossed-legged beside her; a casual conversation lasted only about two to five minutes. But whatever surface dialogue between them had no sign of Ted's inner monologue as the monster was thrilled for a new potential victim.

A girl sat with her two high school friends close to where Janice had chosen to lay out. Sylvia Valint, fifteen, with her classmates were not even two feet away and heard bits of the conversation. They'd seen Janice Ott arrive and become situated, overhearing the conversation between the pair. Sylvia would not be the only one to notice the strange British accent that lingered in Ted's voice. She heard Janice introduce herself as "Jan" but more importantly, she heard the man introduce himself as "Ted." A mistake that would lead to his downfall.

After agreeing to go with Ted under the circumstances that she met his parents, Janice packed up her things and followed him. Numerous witnesses saw the handsome, slim man with his arm in a cast. And as they walked past hundreds of people, not one of them knew to stop Janice, to warn her that once she sat in the passenger seat of that brown Volkswagen her life was about to end.

He wouldn't risk driving for long, it would be a short trip, somewhere he'd thought of before. He'd keep the conversation light, helped ease her nerves. Nothing that would make her appear more human in Ted's eyes. She was his plaything, an object of his possession, and it would be impossible for Janice Ott to escape.

But he was not done for the day. The monster within needed more.

At the exact moment, Janice Ott was being driven away to her death, Denise Naslund, nineteen, was with her boyfriend, Kenny Little, and friends at a Seattle tavern grabbing some lunch before they headed off to Lake Sam. She was enjoying herself now. Denise had an exam coming up the next day for one of her computer programming classes. It was supposed to be a quiet Sunday afternoon after a long weekend of partying. That was until Kenny received a call from their friends Nancy Battema and Bob Sargent, who invited Denise Naslund and Kenny to join them at Lake Sam. Denise was at first hesitant, but she obliged to make Kenny happy.

With striking dark eyes and long brown hair to match, Denise was used to turning heads. She and Nancy often went out to bars, where potential suitors would make their pass at Denise. She would give in and would dance with them. Nothing more. She enjoyed the attention and going out. It was known among her friends, Denise used drugs recreationally, specifically downers. They left the tavern then. She and her friends each took a few Valium in her tan Chevy before arriving at the park. They'd even brought along Little's small dog. Around 1:00 pm they were under the sun and in the massive crowds, eating snacks from the concession. They found a place to share a few beers they'd brought in an ice cooler and passed around a joint. Music from a nearby band played near them.

But Ted was present, lurking about the crowds. He'd come back from wherever he'd left a beaten and weary Janice Ott. At approximately 4:00 pm, he began to approach young women. He told them the same story about needing help with a sailboat. He did this several times. Nervous energy surrounded him. He was desperate to capture another. A junkie needing his fix. He continued scanning the crowds. It was only a matter of time until another woman took his plea and offered aid.

As Ted's monster rose through him, the heat of summer did as well; it approached the nineties. Denise was feeling the full effects of the four valiums she'd taken earlier along with the hot sun, and she grew tired. She told Nancy she was high, and at 4:00 pm, she fell asleep on the beach towel beside her friends. Shortly after getting hotdogs and hamburgers from the food stands, Kenny had trouble waking Denise up to eat, but they sat around and talked. At 4:15 pm, Kenny Little dozed off. Denise stayed up and continued chatting with Nancy under the warm sun. It was 4:40 pm. She rose slowly from the towel, taking care to steady herself. The beer and valium were still working in her system. She didn't bother to wake up her boyfriend or tell Bob and Nancy where she was headed. This wasn't unusual. It was assumed Denise was on her way to the bathroom or to find Kenny's dog, who'd wandered off in the park.

Denise would in fact be seen in her cut off shorts and navy blue halter top, leaving the bathroom only to be approached by a man. It is unknown what exactly Ted said to coax her to his Volkswagen, but it can easily be assumed it was the same tactic he used on Janice Ott. Denise was known for being a kind, caring soul among her friends. It wouldn't be unlike her to help someone, especially a handsome young man like Bundy. He'd found his next possession and just like that, Denise was taken, never to be seen again.

Kenny Little rose thirty minutes later. He sensed something was amiss immediately. Denise had left her purse in the trunk of the car, and she was nowhere to be found. They began their search into the evening, when the massive crowds began to disperse. The darkness of night came; there was still no sign of Denise. They shouted her name, asked people if they'd seen their friend. She was gone. It was Denise's mother who later made the missing person report that night. She hadn't let Kenny finish the story before she ran to the phone to call the police. She knew her daughter was gone, and it was not by choice.

The following afternoon, Janice Ott's roommate would report her missing, and suddenly a family-friendly day in the park had become the scene of a nightmare. Two women had been taken in the brightness of the day. Thousands of eyes and ears around, and yet they'd vanished with only the name Ted as a clue.

Janice Ott and Denise Naslund did not return. A metaphorical storm began brewing in law enforcement as well as the public eye. The searches began, scuba teams dove into the lake, but nothing turned up. There were no bodies to be found. And with each passing minute, it became more and more evident that these two women had faced the same fate as the six others.

That July Sunday evening, Liz Kloepfer left Carkeek Park where she had spent the day. She'd thought perhaps Ted may decide to show up last minute, as he'd expressed his interest in her that morning. Disappointed, she hopped into the shower, washing away the sweat from the day under the sun. But as soon as she stepped out Ted was home. He'd stuck to his plans to continue for dinner. He flopped himself into a chair and waited while she got ready. He was exhausted, and it was apparent. Liz was over the moon to have him over. She immediately noticed he'd developed a cold. She inquired about his day, and he told her two lies. The first was that he'd been cleaning his car, something he'd been known to do constantly. The second was he helped his landlords with yard work.

They had burgers for dinner at a bowling alley. He devoured two large ones then insisted upon getting ice cream. Bundy had exerted himself. The exhaustion was taking its toll. He'd spent the hot July day hunting, and the act of sexual violence and murder drained him. Sleep was his method to reboot, and he needed it desperately. Liz noticed the shift in her Ted after committing two murders as he sat across from her. "As I looked at him across the table, I was struck by how close together his eyes looked. They were a little puffy from his cold, but it was odd that I had never noticed it before."

Even though Ted had assumed he'd gotten away with two murders in the light of day, many witnesses watched the scenes unfold. And to the police, the report of a handsome man with a cast looking for help continued to be reported over and over. Ted Bundy hadn't flown under the radar as much as he'd hoped. He'd also left behind his name "Ted" and the brown

Volkswagen. Now the police, albeit not a conclusive one, had some sort of lead to go off of. They asked witnesses to come forward if they saw this "Ted." They were encouraged to also call or mail in any information or possible tips. At the forefront of the King County investigation to catch this phantom killer was the young Robert D. Keppel. With only a single homicide under his belt, Keppel was about to be thrown into one of the most important manhunts in America's crime history.

Unbeknownst to Liz, Ted had taken that past Thursday and Friday off and would take Monday and Tuesday off as well. He needed time to recover. The weekend drained him, and the cold was in full force. But he returned to work on Wednesday. By then there was enough time for the police to have finished their composite drawing of "Ted." Upon arriving at Washington's Department of Emergency Service for Wednesday, his co-workers joked with him about the similarities between the composite in the newspaper and their friend Ted.

But Ted Bundy's friends weren't the only ones who drew the comparison. A friend and coworker saw the composite. He brought it to Liz. "Don't you think this looks like someone you know?" he asked her. "Doesn't your Ted have a VW?"

Liz didn't want to believe it at first. It couldn't be her Ted, but she had trouble denying the similarities in the drawing. It did in fact resemble Ted Bundy as well as the description of the Volkswagen. The fear began to build. She eventually decided to call in, but like so many other worried wives and girlfriends calling in about their men, nothing came of Liz's call. She worried if her boyfriend was this killer, but also she worried about what would come of him leaving. There were only a few months left until he was off to Utah.

She wasn't the only one to call in Theodore Robert Bundy. Detective Robert Keppel spoke with one of the psychology professors from Puget Sound who identified Ted Bundy saying, "I have a weird guy in my class who drives a 1968 Volkswagen and who matches the composite drawing from your office." A coworker would also call and identify Ted. Though the law student with a perfect record did not fit the bill, the calls had him moved to a special list of potential suspects.

Ted was aware of the police's investigation. He read every article he could to stay one step ahead of them. He figured while they searched for him in Washington then he'd be able to find a new killing ground. One that hadn't heard of this "Ted." But Bundy's arrogance was beginning to blind him. These detectives wouldn't stop until he was caught, and they would follow him, hundreds of miles if they needed too.

And so it was time for Theodore Robert Bundy to leave for Utah. On his last day, he and Liz shared breakfast with friends and packed his VW. She cried as they kissed goodbye. He climbed into his car, driving away with one last look and wave to his love, and then, he was gone.

Not even several days later at Issaquah, a hunter trekking through the forest came across the dried bones and ligaments of Denise Naslund and Janice Ott. One of Ted's dumping grounds was now found, and the worst these detectives now feared was true.

For Theodore Robert Bundy, his killing spree was just beginning. A whole new landscape of opportunity awaited him now, and it was merely a drive away.

The Next Move

Loaded up and on his way to start his second attempt at law school, Ted left Seattle and headed to Salt Lake City, Utah. Gas receipts placed the killer on the road on September 2, 1974. Labor Day. He traveled down 84, driving east. He arrived in Nampa and called Liz, updating her on his venture. His tone was sweet as the two of them reminisced. Boise was not far away. He did not want to delay the trip; therefore, Ted did not speak to her for long.

But Ted Bundy's arrival at Idaho's capitol was delayed. A young woman stood at the top of a freeway on-ramp. In the early evening light, she caught Ted's eye. He saw she was pretty with her green backpack thrown over her shoulder and light brown hair. A hitchhiker who was most likely on her way to Wyoming. Perfect for Ted to sweep off her feet. These were the easiest killings for him. It would be almost impossible to link her back to Ted. A young stranger from a different city, later described by Ted as being about sixteen or eighteen years old.

His beige Volkswagen Beetle pulled into the emergency lane to meet the beautiful hitchhiker. He casually motioned for her to hop in. The young woman probably peered into the car to meet the gaze of her predator. She noticed his handsome face and warm, encouraging smile. His tactful charm eliminated the girl's worries.

The drive began as one normally does. They started chatting away about simple things, introductions, and such. All the while she unknowingly joined him for the most dangerous ride of her young life.

After driving for a while, Ted stopped for gas once more outside of Boise. The evening dipped into the blackness of night. For three hours they continued along, where the road met cut-offs and older highways. He eyed the river that moved along the road. It was perfect terrain for what Bundy's mind and heart sought, and so he made his move. He seized the moment.

Perhaps a rise of fear engulfed the innocent hitchhiker as her driver turned from the highway and onto one of the cut-offs.

The pleasant car ride quickly shifted into panic and manic disarray.

Bundy's fingers carefully reached beneath the seat to find the crowbar he kept stashed away for times like this. The cold metal pressed against his skin as he lifted it, the weight of the weapon held by his arm. Ted was careful to keep it hidden from the passenger's line of sight.

The young hitchhiker may have been frozen with alarm. She might have been too afraid to speak up, too apprehensive to ask her driver the reason for a detour. Or, she could have asked him why only to have Ted remain ominously silent. Her heart would have been pounding. Her pulse would have rung in her ears as the sudden rush of adrenaline hit her system.

In one swift strike, Ted's preferred instrument of death slammed against the young woman's skull. She was knocked out, but still alive. Exactly how Ted loved to have them. Not dead, but incapacitated. He could still have his fun without his prey resisting, similar to a spider with a little fly caught in the web.

It was a perfect time of night, no other cars or people were seen through the shadows cast by the moonlight. He stopped the vehicle, dragged her body out of the car, and stripped her clothes away. Aroused and excited, he raped her, finishing her life with strangulation. After he took her life, Ted would take some time to admire what he had done. He loved the way his victims looked in the new state of death. Perhaps he committed several more sexual acts with the corpse, but he would not linger for too long. He could not save her head nor revisit the sight of murder as he had with his other victims. So instead, he brought her body to the cold water of the river to be taken away, along with her clothes Satisfied with his work, Ted left the riverbank with a flashlight to guide him back to his car. Her identification he would burn, forget her name. As for her green backpack, he'd toss it out of the window of his car leaving it to be found by animals, treating it as he did her body. Disposable.

In the first hours of the morning, he'd finally arrived at 565 First Avenue. His second-floor apartment was close to the University of Utah. Tired from the drive as well as the murder, Ted made his way up the stairs and into his new home. First, he was sure to call Liz to let her know that he made it safely and that he loved his new place.

During the first five days, Ted began to settle in. Meanwhile, an unsuspecting woodsman, Elzie Hammons, found the two bodies of Denise Naslund and Janice Ott, along with an unidentified third set of remains. As Bundy planned, the remains were eaten away by the animals of the heavily wooded area. Their anatomy scattered about.

Detective Robert Keppel led the team of volunteers who swept through one of Bundy's graveyards, searching like a needle in a haystack for any extra clues or missing persons. Keppel claimed the Issaquah crime scene had around 400 pieces of evidence. The painstaking search revealed the history of Ted Bundy and the horrifying acts he took. Years later, Bundy disclosed that Georgeann Hawkins was the third body found in the mountainous graveyard. But even with the discovery of the Issaquah burial site, the King County Police were nowhere near finding their killer. The location did not reveal a motive. Without the motive, a suspect was difficult to pinpoint.

Safely distanced from Ted's makeshift Issaquah cemetery, Bundy began to establish himself among his neighbors and other law students. Although, his professors noted his subsequent lack of attendance. Bundy was never around yet maintained decent grades by performing well on tests.

It was impossible for Ted to attend school full time and still have the freedom to feed his murderous passions to the extent he desired. As the warm September crept into the cool November, Bundy killed at least four young women in a six week period. His drive and need to inflict violence and pain on others consumed him. It claimed his mind, leaving hardly any room for anything else, especially his schoolwork. The act of murders exhausted him. As long as his grades stayed above water, the killer had no reason to go to class, and why would he? There were so many beautiful co-eds around him. In the state of Utah, Bundy was far from the investigation and Washington police. The disappearances and murders were nothing more than a faint whisper to him here.

Here, the real fun could begin.

The day was October 2, 1974. Nancy Wilcox, sixteen, disappeared from Holladay, Utah, just outside of Salt Lake. Pretty, blonde, and a cheerleader, Nancy was last seen by some witnesses riding in what was described as a yellow VW. At first, it was dismissed that she was a runaway. There was no evidence pointing toward foul play, and the police believed she would return home in a short amount of time as most teenagers do.

Little is known behind the true nature of Nancy's disappearance. Her body was never found. Years later, Ted would speak about Miss Wilcox in an interview. He saw her one evening walking along the street. At first, his only intention was to sexually assault her. So he parked his car, bringing a knife with him. He followed her, chasing her into a dark orchard and attempted to take off her clothes. But Nancy put up a struggle. She protested and fought back. He was left with no choice but to cover her mouth with his hand to silence her pleas for help. Once she was quieted, either dead or merely unconscious, Bundy removed her clothes and raped her. He claimed to believe she was only passed out, and he did not know she was dead until he returned to the location to find her body unmoved.

Sixteen days later, the seventeen-year-old daughter of Midvale's police chief disappeared. With hazel eyes and light brown hair, Melissa Smith was known to have a temper when she didn't get her way. She planned to attend a slumber party that evening, but when she called to confirm her plans no one picked up. Melissa, regardless, continued to wait for her ride to the party. They never showed either. Turned out the whole night had been canceled. Unfortunately for Miss Smith, no one thought to tell her the party was called off, and she was understandably upset.

She made new arrangements with her night. Melissa decided to head out of the house and grab some pizza with a girlfriend at a pizzeria. These last minutes plans were going to have to do. Miss Smith and her friend sat at a booth enjoying their cheesy meal. The two young women probably joked and laughed with each other. They may have gossiped about Melissa's difficult night or chatted about potential boyfriends. Whatever their conversation was, they finished their food, paid for their late dinner, and exited the restaurant. Little did the two know, an ominous onlooker watched their every move. One witness would come forward later, believing to have seen Ted Bundy sitting behind her booth, exiting almost immediately after her.

Melissa called her home around nine to let her family know she'd be out until around 10:00 pm.

But Melissa never returned home. Instead, at around 10:15 pm a witness finished up some late-night yard work. They raked leaves in the twilight, and suddenly heard a scream from a distance. Their home was along the route Melissa would have taken to return to her family. One that Ted Bundy must have lurked in the shadows, waiting.

In Wasatch County, Melissa's body was uncovered, partially frozen, and nude in the woods. One of her blue knee-length stockings had been turned into a ligature and tied around her neck. Cuts and scrapes from being dragged a far distance covered her skin. But those injuries did not compare to her skull. She had sustained a great deal of damage. Melissa had been struck several times with something hard, possibly a crowbar.

Strangely her eye makeup was in pristine condition, her nails freshly painted, and her hair washed. There was no sign of a struggle. Shockingly enough, the state of her body revealed to detectives that Melissa Smith had only died thirty to thirty-six hours since being found, which meant she was alive and held somewhere by her captor for five days before dying. Due to her head injuries, she was unconscious for the duration her captor had her. Where exactly he kept her during this time is not known, but Melissa's sister admitted that the makeup did not belong to Melissa. This monster had used her as some sort of doll, to dress up and play with however he desired.

Back in Utah, Liz Kloepfer's friend named Angie made her way from Washington to visit family that October. She'd left an anxious Liz who was unsure of what her dear boyfriend was doing. At night she had no choice but to lie in bed and wonder. As Angie made her way over, she heard news over the radio that hunters had found the body of Melissa Smith. "I don't want to scare you, but it's happening in Utah right now," Angie told Liz afterward. It was inevitable. Suspicion crept into Liz's heart. She feared the worst.

Liz called the King County Police. She spoke with detectives, determined to help them catch the man responsible for these killings. If it was her Ted doing it, then she would help stop it all. But the call may have become overwhelming. She told the officers about her situation without ever revealing Ted Bundy's name. She protected him by not sharing his true identity. Maybe a part of her did not want to let him go from her life. In the phone call, she talked about the Volkswagen and how the same murders happening in Washington were beginning in Utah.

Halloween night, another young woman disappeared in Utah. Laura Aimes was seventeen years old and known to be a free spirit. Her parents weren't always informed of where she was. She was a typical teenager and not a fan of rules. Standing at almost six feet tall and weighing around 140 pounds, Laura was somewhat of a tomboy. She enjoyed riding horses, being outdoors, and hunting with her father. Her wandering spirit and confidence gave her little to fear. She'd recently quit school and was living with a friend. But she contacted her parents every now and then to check-in. With the disappearance of Melissa Smith lingering in the news, Laura's mother warned her daughter of the dangers that came with hitchhiking, but Laura was fearless. Those disappearances were something that happened on the news, not to someone like her.

On the cool Halloween night of 1974, Laura left a house party in Orem. She had plans to hitchhike back to a nearby city to pick up some cigarettes and potentially look for something more interesting to do with her night.

Something more interesting did happen.

Laura left the party to begin her next move, but Bundy was there, ready to offer her that ride only to take her life. Laura was not seen alive after that night.

A little over a week later, Bundy needed to indulge again. In the Fashion Place Mall located in Murray, Utah on Friday, November 8, 1974, a young woman stood in front of the Waldenbooks store window. Carol DaRonch had stopped by the mall after work that evening to pick up a birthday gift. The busy Christmas shoppers swarmed around her in between the shops. She turned to re-enter the Sears store when she was stopped by what she described as a man who looked better than average and well-groomed. He wore dark green pants and a dress jacket. He identified himself as "Officer Roseland."

The so-called officer asked Carol DaRonch if she had a car parked in the Sear's parking lot. She confirmed that she did, having parked outside one of the anchor stores, which seemed to be of no serious consequences. The officer informed her that they believed a suspect had attempted to break into her car and that she should come with him to see if there was any damage or if anything had gone missing. She agreed. The story seemed fairly believable. Together they walked through the mall to where Carol parked her car. The light misty rain came down around them in the early evening in the wide parking lot.

She noticed how the officer walked ahead of her with haste, taking long strides for his steps. But to the confusion of the eighteen-year-old, her Camaro was completely fine. She inspected the outside. She told the officer there was no damage, and she opened the driver door and glanced in. Nothing was out of place. He asked her to open the passenger door as well, but Carol was not completely buying it. Something seemed off with this so-called policeman. She told Officer Roseland there was no need. She insisted her car was fine.

Perhaps that was the moment Bundy had planned to attack DaRonch, but her refusal of his commands ruined his plot. The fake officer was put on the spot. He adjusted, asking her to join him back in the mall where Bundy's alleged partner waited, holding the said suspect. He told Carol that she needed to report a complaint against him. They returned to the mall, but the officer was unable to locate his partner. This was, of course, because there wasn't one. Instead, Bundy continued pushing his luck with the farce. He asked Carol DaRonch to follow him to the police station which was luckily right across the road from the mall. She agreed, and they moved through the sea of people. Though her suspicion rose slightly, she still had no reason to completely doubt the policeman. He was kind, and his demeanor was cool.

He led her across the street, maintaining the guise well. But he did not bring her to a police station. Inside it was a laundromat. The door was locked, and Bundy played it off. He knew the door would be bolted shut, and he told DaRonch she would have to come with him to the Main Police Station. DaRonch's guard rose slightly. She asked him for some form of identification. Bundy was prepared. Quickly, he removed his billfold and flashed a badge. She was unable to get a close look before he slipped it into his back pocket. She was unable to recall whether it was gold or silver.

With that reassurance of the man's story, they made their way to his Volkswagen Beetle. He climbed in, buckling his seat, telling her to do the same, but a second time Carol refused his commands. He turned the ignition after making sure that the passenger door was locked. As the car pulled out of the parking lot, Carol was surprised to see that Bundy was not heading for the police station. He drove in the complete opposite direction. Until this moment, she kept a safe distance from the man. Closer to each other inside of the car, she smelled the sour stench of alcohol lingering on his breath.

She barely had any time to ask him what he was doing before Bundy jerked the car over and parked it in front of a grade school then attacked Carol. She now battled for her life. Her fingers reached for the handle of the door, grasping. She managed to open it slightly, as the hard metal clamp of handcuffs slammed around her wrist. Screams passed her lips. "What are you doing... what are you doing... let me go!" She thrashed beneath him, kicking and scratching with all of her strength, breaking her fingernails. She put up a fight and in the struggle, Bundy made the mistake of only getting one wrist in the cuff while the other dangled freely. They were useless, and Carol was given a real chance. In the dimness of the light, Bundy pulled a gun out and told her "I'll blow your head off." Carol wished for death then, but she would not give up the fight. And in the dark, moonless night, she saw the soulless eyes of a cold killer.

Ted Bundy lost Carol. She escaped from his grasp, bursting out of the car; she screamed. Running wildly down the street, Carol sprinted with a primal drive. One of her shoes flew off, and her arms waved. A hungry predator chased after her.

The headlights of an approaching car came closer. Wilbur Walsh and his wife, Mary, were shocked to see the fearful, hysterical woman waving them down. They had no chance of making sense of any of it before Carol jumped into their car. "I can't believe it. I can't believe it... a man... a man... he was going to kill me." Carol repeated as her body shook and the fear continued to overwhelm her. At first the Walsh's were in a panic, but then they realized Carol needed help desperately. "When I saw the state this child was in, I realized it couldn't be anything harmful to me. It was harmful to her. I have never seen a human being that frightened in my life. She was trembling and crying and weak, as if she was going to faint. She was in a terrible state," Mary recalled. They rushed her to the police station, where they stayed with the young woman, comforting her through the realization that her life had almost been taken that very night.

But what shocked Carol the most, was what she learned later on. Because she was able to escape from Ted Bundy, he immediately became overwhelmed with rage. Anger from losing control of his prey. The inability to complete his pursuit motivated him more than anything to kill that night, only hours later.

Having lost his possession, Ted was livid. He had come far too close to not quench his demonic thirst that night. Bundy racked his mind for where to find his next toy. His thoughts turned to the high school play he recalled finding a brochure about on Monday, October 28. For Ted, his night was not a complete loss. In Bountiful, Viewmont Highschool's production of the musical, *The Redhead,* was only a short drive away. His chase for Carol ended, and he was quickly back in the Volkswagen speeding away to find his next victim.

1,500 people had come that night to watch Viewmont's production. The sheer number of witnesses would not deter Bundy. On the contrary, in plain sight was where he hid best. Or at least he thought. He parked his car outside the auditorium concealed from light, always thankful for the cover of the shadows. He entered the main front doors of the auditorium, scanning for his new possession. He approached twenty-four-year-old Raelynne Shepard, the Viewmont Highschool drama teacher. At first, he said nothing more than a curt greeting. The second time he approached her, he complimented her beautiful eyes and later on asked her to join him in the parking lot to help identify a vehicle. She was far too busy with readying the musical to stop and help the man, but she did take note of how well-dressed he was. She noticed his patent leather shoes.

No matter. Ted was only beginning his search. He had all night. The chase was as thrilling as the hunt, but Carol's escape tried his patience.

The Kent family arrived and were taking their seats. Their seventeen-year-old daughter, a senior at Viewmont, was excited about the show, but the whole family was not present. Her younger brother did not attend. He had been dropped off at the roller rink to be picked up after the musical.

Raelynne continued to notice the strange, well-dressed man throughout the night. She did not think much about it until she continued seeing him. She approached him, asking if he received the help he was searching for. But the man did not respond. Ted Bundy only stared oddly. At this moment, he may have been listening to what he would later describe as a growling voice that overtook his thoughts with the instructions of what he should do to his prey. But as Raelynne continued on to the auditorium, the fashionable man sparked in her a peculiar feeling of unease.

Before intermission, Raelynne once more encountered Ted Bundy. As she made her way to help facilitate a costume change, Ted approached her boldly. He touched her arm, grabbing her attention. His focus was more on her breasts than her eyes. He made the remark that he'd been watching her all night, and he really needed her to come to identify a car. He commented about how much he loved long hair. Immediately put off by the strange and creepy display of behavior, Raelynne pushed him away and continued to the dressing room. During intermission, she saw him leave. She was glad to have him gone, but Ted never left.

The play started later than scheduled, and the Kent family realized they would be late to pick up their son. Debbie got up to call the roller rink and let her brother know the change in plans. But the rink refused to page her brother nor relay a message. Debbie offered to go and get her brother while her parents stayed at the auditorium. She wanted them to enjoy the rest of the show.

Ted reappeared. Toward the end of the show, Raelynne saw the man once more, he sat directly behind the Kents.

Ted had made his way to the back of the auditorium during intermission. He paced back and forth along the wall in a disheveled, messy state. His hair was tousled, and his clothes haphazardly draped on his frame. He breathed heavily. He appeared to be like a junky unable to get his fix. Desperate and dangerous. At some point, his eyes fell upon Debbie Kent as she sat near the back row with her parents. He would not miss the young woman leaving and heading to her car to get her brother. He, without a doubt, followed her out into the parking lot. At some point, perhaps he lured her closer to his vehicle or enraged and frustrated he simply overpowered her rendering her unconscious before throwing her into his car.

Either way, as the curtain fell and the students took their last bows, Debbie Kent never arrived to pick up her brother, nor did she return to the auditorium.

One witness saw a Volkswagen Beetle speeding away from Viewmont High School's parking lot. Undoubtedly it was Ted, whisking away Debbie Kent. And as for the poor family, it was a terrible night that only grew worse.

On the following Saturday, early morning, the Bountiful Police Department searched the parking lot of the high school only to find a key. A key that would belong to a pair of handcuffs one woman was put into during an attempted kidnapping not even an hour away. It was the perfect fit for the handcuffs put on Carol DaRonch.

Almost twenty days later, on November 27, 1974, two students from Brigham Young University would uncover the remains of Laura Ann Aimes in the American Fork Canyon. Her skull had suffered severe blunt trauma, a deep cut ran along the back of her head and a stocking tied tightly around her neck. At first, some thought it was Debbie Kent, but that was quickly ruled out. Her autopsy revealed shocking similarities with that of Melissa Smith. She had evidence of both anal and vaginal trauma, including a vaginal wound that may have been inflicted with Bundy's ice pick. Most eerily, Aimes' hair had been freshly shampooed, similar to the nail panting and fresh make-up of Melissa Smith.

Fear, as it had grown in Washington, rose throughout Utah. The peaceful communities were being uprooted by a horrible monster. One they knew very little about.

The Lethal New Year

The desperate fear had not reached the other parts of the U.S. It was time for Ted to travel north where he could continue to feed his insatiable hunger for power and blood without interruption. He could no longer continue his terrible work in Utah. In a little over a month, he had stirred the state into a storm of chaos and trepidation. He needed new hunting grounds.

Of course, since other parts of the U.S. were unaware of the monster lurking on the west side, Caryn Campbell and her family from Michigan would not have heard of the monstrous killer or seen the sketch made by the Washington police. Unaware, the family continued with their holiday plans at the Wildwood Inn near Aspen, Colorado.

Dr. Raymond Gadowski was joined by his girlfriend and two children. Caryn had been with the thirty-one-year-old osteopath for some time, and the two of them were living together for about a year. The rumor of engagement was becoming more of a reality. Caryn was a stunning brunette. The type that turned heads. She, as well as Raymond, was an avid skier. The trip was going to be wonderful, with Raymond attending conferences for a medical event, and Caryn, a nurse herself, skiing with her boyfriend's kids out on the slopes.

January 12, 1975, the day had a great start. Raymond cut out of the conference meeting early to join his girlfriend and kids out on the slopes. They ended everything after dinner at the Snowmass Village. She picked at her food dealing with a light stomachache. She had a glass of milk with her stew.

The winter chill was in full strength, dropping down far below freezing. Caryn had left her purse and room key in their suite. As the night began to wind down, they ended in the lobby of the hotel, resting by the fire. Caryn purchased a magazine early that day and asked Raymond if he would go and retrieve the magazine for her to read. She and a fellow friend made a joke to trade magazines, his being a *Playboy* and hers a *Viva*.

For whatever reason, whether it be that he was too tired or in a bad mood, Raymond refused to go to the room for Caryn.

He'd rather stay by the fire with his kids. This decision cost Caryn her life. Turning on her heels, Caryn made her way back to the room. A witness remembered her getting off the elevator of the second floor, where her room was. But that was the last time Caryn was ever seen.

Raymond waited in the lobby. The minutes began to pass. Caryn left with the promise of a prompt return and yet, she never came back. After waiting for a while, longer than it should have taken to quickly grab a magazine, Raymond with his children made their way back to room 210. There he found Caryn's purse. The issue of *Viva* remained untouched. She'd never made it back to the room. He passed by the cocktail party as well as returning to the Snowmass Village, but there was no sign of Caryn. Raymond immediately contacted the police.

An hour before midnight, the police arrived. They asked the typical questions and documented the normal information. Hearing about the dispute over the magazine, the police suggested Caryn was possibly upset and would perhaps return.

But Raymond knew better. He knew his girlfriend would not run off like that. Not without a word or grabbing her purse.

The next morning, Michael Fisher, chief criminal investigator for the Ninth Judicial District, State of Colorado, was brought on. He got in his car and made his way to the Wildwood Inn. Unsure of how a disappearance like this could happen at a place like the Wildwood Inn, he thought of possible suspects and put Raymond Gadowski at the top. There was still the possibility, Caryn could have left and would eventually turn up. Strange behavior wasn't foreign to Aspen. It was the cold, snowy state people came to escape the hustle and bustle of their lives.

Fisher was detailed and made his way door to door, knocking in an attempt to gather witnesses' accounts. It went on for a week. He scoured the inn, wondering how a potential disappearance could happen. Based on the layout of the Inn, Fisher came to the conclusion Caryn Campbell's abductor might have willingly lured her away from the public areas. Too many eyes would have seen a violent struggle. Perhaps Ted feigned injury like he had so many times in Washington, preying on Caryn's role as a nurse. She could have been trying to help a man in obvious need.

Bundy knew it made his killings easier if the women willingly left with him. He was a smart killer. Knew how to strike and when. His other strategy included a greater distance between him and the kidnapping location. Bundy would admit years later that he got Caryn in his car and took her away, killing her in his Volkswagen that very night.

Raymond stayed around for a week. He tried his best to maintain his composure for his children, but there was no doubt the guilt continued eating away at his heart. Fisher ruled Raymond out after interviewing him. A polygraph proved inconclusive, but Fisher felt confident Raymond was not the cause for Caryn's sudden disappearance.

Caryn's nude body was found only about 2.8 miles from Wildwood Inn that February, on the 17th. She laid in a snowfield running along a dirt road. The frozen flesh of her face and neck and been picked at by hungry animals. Fisher arrived at the scene and had her body taken in for an autopsy. Her cause of death was blunt force trauma to the back of the head. A tooth had been broken from the impact and based on the partially digested stew and milk in her stomach she'd been killed two to six hours after dinner. It became clear to Fisher solving this murder would be no easy task, but he was not to be discouraged. His investigation would enter a grueling process, for the killer was long gone. But Ted Bundy was not finished with Colorado.

In fact, he was only beginning.

With the fresh winter start and the beginning of Ted's spring semester, he started his second bout of law school with newfound gusto. He wanted to make up for his lack of attendance during the fall. For Bundy, the excitement of a new hunting ground was enough to push him forward. He was no longer under the weight of the Washington police nor the eye of his adoring girlfriend, Liz.

Liz had just finished a Christmas vacation with Ted. Any of the doubt she felt that fall was eliminated when they were reunited. Her daughter Tina was thrilled to see her mother's boyfriend. The normalcy of the reunion began to stir feelings of guilt in Liz. Perhaps she was wrong to have doubted his character. But when he left to continue the killings, Liz was removed from his charming spell, and she'd called the Salt Lake Police. Captain Hayward himself spoke with her, and when she addressed her concerns about Ted Bundy, he assured her that the law student had already been checked out. They had no reason to be suspicious of Ted Bundy.

And so the investigations continued with no clear route to an answer or clue. On March 1, 1975, the second dumpsite on Taylor Mountain, back in Washington, was uncovered. Even more families' hopes in finding their lost children alive were crushed with the reality that these young women would never come home. Keppel and his team scoured the land, looking for any more clues or bone fragments. They uncovered the remains of four women all who suffered at Bundy's hands.

Ted Bundy kept track of the news as it was released, delighting in the police's discovery. It did nothing to deter him. Little did.

On March 14th, it was the start of a new weekend, and the weekend was Bundy's time to kill when he wouldn't have to worry about classes. He jumped on the highway, heading out of Utah. He saw great success at the Wildwood Inn and sought a similar experience for the evening. He found his way to Vail, Colorado.

It was around 9:00 pm when Julie Cunningham, twenty-six, left her small apartment to meet with friends at a nearby tavern. She worked as a ski resort instructor. On that dark, fateful, cold night, Julie would have the misfortune of seeing a struggling Bundy fumble with his ski equipment. He used a crutch as a prop and asked for help from the lovely woman, taking his supplies to the car.

She agreed, and together they made their way. The conversation was full of small talk. Bundy told her about how he hurt his leg in a skiing accident. Then they approached the vehicle. He described the incident later on in an interview. "When I opened the door and she bent over, I hit her in the head and pushed her into the car, she was unconscious, and as I drove away I put handcuffs on her." He exited then, tearing down the highway. "She was unconscious for a short time and then (when) she came to, she was asking where she was, what was this all about." Perhaps her mounting fear and panic pleased Ted and his self-described entity. He knew exactly where they were headed; he had a spot in mind, one along a lake with a thick shield of Juniper trees to obscure the view.

At the location, he wasted no time inflicting the pain and torment on the young woman to get his sexual release. He choked her until she passed out then had sex with her. He left the car door open, waiting for her to wake. When she did, the glimmer of freedom taunted her, and Julie took off bolting out of the car toward the road. But there was no one around in the isolated location, not for miles. Bundy had planned it all. It was all a sick game of cat and mouse. He chased her down, tackling her, then he choked her to death. Her naked body was left underneath those juniper trees, and her personal belongings were to be bagged and tossed out miles away.

He would later revisit the murder site at two different times. Bundy did not disclose what occurred during those visits nor what he hoped to accomplish. Was it to just see his work, or was it to relive the moment? Could it have been to indulge in another sexual fantasy? Regardless of his mission, on the second visit, he buried the body.

Without skipping a beat, Ted Bundy returned to Utah, jumping back into attending classes and making sure to keep in touch with Liz. Business as usual.

On Friday, April 4th, Bundy was back in Colorado and on the prowl. He visited the site of Julie Cunningham's murder. Bundy often revisited the places of the murder as well as the places the bodies were buried. It was a sacred place for him. A place to remember what he'd done and relive those horrifying moments that he savored.

On April 6, he drove through to Grand Junction, Colorado. Even a small, sleepy town like this was not safe from the dangers of the prowling monster. It didn't take long until Ted was engrossed in another victim. The beautiful Denise Oliverson. The petite woman caught his eye while riding her yellow bike in town. She'd left her boyfriend after an argument and chose to head over to her parents. She may have wanted the time to think and enjoy the fresh air.

But it ended with Bundy stopping his car and roping her in, either by brute force or a feigned need of help. After that day, Denise Oliverson was never seen again. She became a quick kill. Her body used for whatever fantasy and desire Ted craved for at that moment then dumped in the Colorado River to be lost forever.

He returned home then, back to his life after satiating his urge. He made sure to send flowers to Liz for her thirtieth birthday. Even with such gestures, Liz's fear and confusion continued to swirl around her. Something was not exactly right. Unable to steal as he normally did, Bundy took up a job working as a custodian, but he missed work and would show up drunk at times. He was fired mid-summer that year.

As Bundy continued slipping into the cloak of normalcy, Mike Fisher continued his hunt. He watched as a similar pattern of killings unfolded in Colorado similar to that of Utah. He phoned Salt Lake City's police. They agreed to meet and compare notes. It was obvious there was a shocking similarity in their cases. They were dealing with a single, mobile killer. It was the same person. Fisher would later say, "You couldn't look at those photographs and autopsy slides and read those reports without noting gross similarities. We didn't come back from the meeting saying, 'Okay, we have one man doing all these heinous things.' But we were confident that there was a high degree of probability that we all had the same problem."

On May 5, 1975, the winter chill still lingered even though it was spring, and Bundy was on the move to Idaho. In Pocatello, his eyes fell on the sign for Idaho University. Using a fake name, he paid for a room at the nearby Holiday Inn, ensuring to book a hotel room near the rear of the building. He prowled the campus, even making his way into a women's dormitory where a male authority figure stopped him. He would return to that Holiday Inn, empty-handed. Without a prize, Bundy twisted and writhed. He needed his outlet for release. Without a victim that night, he woke in the morning desperate.

Bundy would later confess to the murder of Lynette Culver, though he would never be officially linked to the case. He hopped into his car and drove, searching until he came to Alameda Junior High school. It was lunchtime and a group of children were outside. Lynette may have been boarding the bus or leaving campus for lunch. His eyes fell on twelve-year-old

Lynette Culver with light brown hair and hazel eyes. He pulled the car up, rolling down his window. The twelve-year-old approached the vehicle, and they spoke to one another. Bundy later claimed he thought she was older. It was clear Bundy charmed the young girl because through the conversation she opened the door and slid right in.

He later would drown the girl in a bathtub. Although he never revealed where nor how. His desire for necrophilia was satisfied. In an interview with Randy Everitt, when asked why he did these things, Bundy simply replied, "It was the madness." And after the murder was completed, Bundy placed Culver's body in the trunk of the car, ensuring no one was around to see and he sped away, dumping her body in a river north of Pocatello.

Her body has never been recovered.

June 6, Bundy arrived in Seattle. He shocked Liz with his unannounced arrival. Together he and Tina planned a surprise dinner for Liz, who was beyond thrilled to have Ted home. He'd come back for her.

But as quickly as he arrived, he would leave. He returned to Utah. June 27, 1975, in the evening fifteen-year-old Susan Curtis was with two other friends. At the Wilkinson Student Center on the campus of Brigham Young University, the girls were attending a banquet for the Bountiful Orchard Youth Conference. Having braces, Susan worried about taking care of her teeth and told her friends that she planned to return to her room to brush them. She left then, going along a path many others were on. It was a seemingly safe route, there was little for the kids to worry about.

Except along the path, Bundy waited. He, by some nefarious means, lured her away off the path and violently assaulted her.

Shelley Robertson's life was taken as well. July 1, She never showed up for work at the printing business her family ran in Golden, Colorado. Her body was found nearly two months later on August 23, 1975. She was left at an old mine shaft near Berthoud Pass. Her naked body had been bound with duct tape with no other evidence for detectives beside the fact Shelley had been murdered and abandoned.

Another murder is often attributed to Bundy at this time but has never been confirmed. He later denied he ever killed her. It took place north of Salt Lake City in Layton. Twenty-three-year old Nancy Baird worked at Fina gas station on a busy fourth of July. The flow of traffic came and went. But at around 5:30 pm Nancy was suddenly not there. Her purse and car were left behind, untouched since she arrived at work. There were no witnesses, no talk of a struggle. Nancy Baird like so many other young women seemingly vanished into thin air. Her body was never recovered.

Monster Unmasked

August 16, 1975. Bundy claimed that evening was an innocent night, he claimed his late-night plans were to merely drive around and smoke dope. "I really didn't know what was on my mind," he told Stephen Michaud about that night, "or what I wanted to do. I was a little bit fucked up."

At 2:30 am, he sat in his VW, joint pressed to his lips. The smoke lingered over the open road map he examined. He enjoyed the high from marijuana. Bright red lights flared in his rearview mirror, ripping him from his peaceful state. Sergeant Bob Hayward of the Utah Highway Patrol was behind Ted Bundy. Burglaries were happening often in Hayward's neighborhood, and the officer feared this could easily be one. It was nothing more than a routine traffic stop, but it took a quick turn.

The sudden flash of the headlights jolted Bundy. Ted's foot slammed down on the clutch then he hit the gas, lurching forward. In his influenced state and the shock of fear, Ted made the mistake of leaving his headlights off. Hayward had a reason to pursue the mysterious parked car.

In a panic, Bundy blew through two stop signs. He dumped the weed out of his window and raced through the subdivisions. Hayward was now in pursuit as Bundy flew as fast as he could down the road. His heart thudded and blood coursed through his veins. Breathing heavily, he found the highway, but there was no chance of escape for the killer. Not now at least. Bundy accepted escape was clearly not happening. He decided then to pull into an empty gas station and work the charm he knew to manage so well. In the meantime, Hayward called for backup. He would not take any chances.

Ted stepped out of the car, dressed in a dark blue turtleneck, jeans, and tennis shoes. After asking to see his license, Bundy obliged with a smile reaching for it out of his car. With his flashlight, Hayward studied the identification. He asked Bundy what he was up to. Bundy first fumbled through a poor alibi. Several other officers showed up to the scene after

Hayward called them in. Ted kept up the air of charm, never wavering, but even so, his evasion of the police and odd collection of items gave the police no doubt this strange man participated in suspicious behavior. This person was up to something. He told them the tale of being at a drive-in movie theatre. He saw *The Towering Inferno*. But no drive-in in the area was playing it. Bundy reiterated he was lost.

But with the flashlight, Hayward peered into the vehicle which held twenty-some murder victims. Immediately, he noticed the passenger seat removed and placed in the back seat. Odd. Then his eyes led him to more ominous findings. On the floor was a brown gym bag. Its contents included a seven-inch nylon rope, a ski mask, a cotton glove with a leather handgrip, a Sears model 6577 pry bar, a black leather ski glove, a pair of pantyhose with eyes and nose holes removed, Glad trash bags, a flashlight, piece of orange wire, an ice pick with a red handle, and strips of white cloth differing in length. Later, a pair of handcuffs were found in the trunk of the car.

Hayward arrested him that night on the charge of "Attempting to Evade a Police Officer." He was taken in around 3:30 am.

Bundy was brought to jail for the first time for violating traffic laws and the suspected burglary kit. He was photographed and released, but his gym bag full of the tools for murder was taken away, never to be seen by Bundy again. He was enraged by the police taking him in. Bundy reasoned he'd been doing nothing wrong that night, but his hate and lack of respect for policemen was evident.

Bundy went home, walking back to his apartment. To the homicide detectives desperately chasing for a murderer with mysterious motives, Bundy's arrest was one massive step toward progress. That following Tuesday, detectives from the surrounding counties gathered to discuss updates, cases, and suspects. Detective Jerry Thompson from the Salt Lake County Sheriff's Office attended. The news about Bundy's recent arrest and possession of burglary tools immediately grabbed his attention. He'd heard Bundy's name before. The mention of the Volkswagen and handcuffs especially piqued his interest. He called Carol DaRonch and discussed the handcuffs used on her. There was more than what meets the eye with Ted Bundy. Detective Jerry Thompson could feel it.

The meeting ended. Thompson immediately returned to his office. He looked up the information they had on Theodore Robert Bundy. He'd kept a stack of alphabetized cards of suspects and quickly searched through it. The initial info on Bundy came when the law student made his move to Salt Lake City from Detective Robert Keppel of Washington. Keppel wanted to inform the Utah authorities and Jerry Thompson the potential suspect was on the move. But during this call Keppel and Jerry Thompson agreed they both did not suspect Bundy. His record was clean, and his background did not fit their profile.

But this late night arrest changed Thompson's opinion. Quickly.

Jerry Thompson's partner contacted the Seattle authorities. As the call came in, Detective Robert Keppel and his team had moved on to the next suspect in their list of 100 potential Teds to further investigate. The next name on the list was Bundy's.

Hearing of his arrest on August 16, Liz decided to end their engagement. She contacted the police once more.

Detective Jerry Thompson would not hold back on his investigation into Bundy. It was becoming clearer every day this was their guy. Thompson would do whatever it took to get the answers and truth from Bundy. He knew that if Bundy was the perpetrator then Carol DaRonch would be able to identify him. Hopefully.

August 21, Utah police fulfilled their wish in finding Ted Bundy. Ted spent his afternoon refinishing an oak table he'd stolen. His upstairs apartment was full of luxurious stolen goods. The detectives knew something more sinister lurked behind those bright blue eyes. It unsettled even the most seasoned of police. Bundy was not a typical burglar. He did not fit the usual profile. Regardless, they made their way to his apartment, pulling up. Bundy greeted the police to be immediately met with an arrest warrant. He was allowed to switch clothes before the handcuffs met his wrists, and he was again on his way to jail within a week of his last arrest. Bundy remained calm, and the detectives were slightly confused by the nice persona of the mask Bundy wore.

Upon being brought in, Bundy was taken in for questioning. At first, Ted felt overly confident. He had no problem defending himself against the police. They told Ted that they wanted to know about the burglar tools found in his car. Bundy was relieved. He was in no real danger. Instead of asking for a lawyer or refusing to speak, he wanted to have a game of wits. He thought he was better than the detectives, but he caught himself in several white lies, unable to remember what little details slipped out about what. He'd already messed up the lie about how he obtained the handcuffs, telling two different stories to two different officers. But the detectives wanted Bundy to know that it wasn't burglary they were interviewing him for like Bundy originally thought. "My game is homicide!" Detective Forbes snapped suddenly in the small room. The news startled Bundy. He was then handed a paper that if signed would allow the police access to search his apartment. Bundy agreed, signing the release.

They left to search his apartment. Jerry Thompson joined them surprised by the level of tidiness in the home. Everything had its place, being organized in a neat and orderly fashion. Not a speck of dirt could be found, nor an article of clothing out of place. Bundy sat, restrained on the couch as his apartment was searched. Two policemen stood over him. Drawers opened and shelves inspected. Bundy attempted to keep the conversation going, but not out of anxiety. No. No one could see an ounce of fear in him about being discovered. His guilty conscience already knew the reason, but he never openly showed it.

Several items of note were found in Bundy's Utah apartment. They included the following: a road map for Colorado, a Colorado Ski Country Guide '74 and '75, a Bountiful Recreation Center brochure, as well as a copy of a phone bill dated for June. A call had been made to Denver, Colorado. When asked by Jerry Thompson about Colorado. Bundy said he'd never been to the state nor knew anyone there. Thompson pushed the questioning about the Colorado items. He wanted to know how Bundy came to have them. "They were left here," he said, "by a friend of mine who was talking about how good the skiing was over there." And when asked about the Bountiful brochure Bundy simply replied, "Is that the city just north of Salt Lake? I've heard about it, and probably driven through it, but I've never been there to speak of." He lied through his teeth with a forced smile. The brochure was in fact an advertisement for the Viewmont musical. Before they left, they photographed the VW, shooting the inside and out of the car. The search was completed, and Bundy returned to jail.

But Bundy made bail, and with the help of his new defense attorney, John O'Connell, he was out of the hands of the law enforcement. For now.

Detective Jerry Thompson made his way to Murray, Utah, on Monday, the first of September. With him, he brought the Polaroids of Bundy's car as well as a stack of images of potential suspects. Thompson was on his way to see Carol DaRonch, who would become his star witness. After chatting a bit, he showed her the images of the Volkswagen. She told him there were strong resemblances; she even identified a tear in the passenger's seat. Then he gave her the stack of potential suspects. She took her time examining the images. Without saying a word, she pulled Bundy's picture out and set it upon her lap. She did not draw attention to it until she'd finished, then handed Thompson back the photos. "I don't see anyone in there," she said. Thompson inquired about Bundy's picture. The one still kept in her fist. She'd forgotten about that one. "I don't know, it looks something like him. I really don't know, I can't be sure, but it does look a lot like him." At the end of their meeting, she promised Thompson to come to a lineup. He left her then, satisfied with their talk. If Carol identified Ted Bundy in the lineup, then they were one step closer to finding answers.

Carol wasn't the only one to recognize Bundy. His mugshot was used to show the Viewmont High School drama teacher, who agreed that Bundy's mugshot matched the man who was seen slinking around the auditorium on the day of Debbie Kent's disappearance. Witnesses from Lake Sammamish also identified the images of Ted as being the man under the hot sun that day.

September 8, Fisher reached out to Jerry Thompson with the information that not only had Bundy been in Colorado, but his gas receipts matched locations where victims disappeared as well as the dates they vanished. He'd gotten gas in Vail, Colorado, the day Julie Cunningham disappeared. The pieces lined up. Thompson pushed deeper in his investigation. He arrived at the University of Utah to find Bundy's records and speak with his professors. Bundy found out about this and decided to follow Thompson around the campus. For Bundy, it was a game, and he believed he was smarter than the detectives. He even taunted Thompson with sarcastic remarks.

Bundy's arrogance blinded him from the reality that he was no match for the three lead investigators hunting him down, Robert Keppel from Seattle, Mike Fisher in Aspen, and Jerry Thompson of Salt Lake. And on October 1, Thompson arrived at the doorstep of Bundy's apartment. Thompson revealed the subpoena to Bundy who visibly became shaken, but it was only for a lineup. Bundy regained his composure. He hadn't been accused of murder, not yet.

He figured this would be an easy thing to get out of. And the ever calculated Bundy immediately got dressed after the detectives left, grabbed his keys, and went to have a haircut. He needed to change his appearance, something he'd mastered through the years. His hair had been long and bushy, so he opted for a short clean cut. His new look ebbed away any real concern.

He'd look similar to the other men standing beside him. He'd little to fear, especially with his new look. But Bundy's arrogance once again blinded him.

Bundy arrived the next morning, October 2nd, for the scheduled line up. Thomas was immediately rattled with the transformation. He hoped it wouldn't deter Carol away from her original gut reaction. But he feared his case might be abandoned before it ever started.

The witnesses came. Raelynne Shepard, Tamara Tingey, a girl who shared a locker with Debbie Kent, and Carol DaRonch. Even with the haircut, all the women identified him immediately. Bundy was shocked by the news. He'd thought surely he'd evaded the lineup. And on that day, he was charged with kidnapping and attempted murder. His bail was set to $100,000. It was later dropped to $15,000.

The news of Bundy's arrest spread throughout. His friends and family were shocked to hear it all. They were confused. It had to be impossible that the Ted they knew and loved would be responsible for such heinous activities. But no one was affected by the news as much as Elizabeth Kloepfer. Confusion filled her head. She had her doubts, but to have the news confirmed broke her. Her heart filled with conflict. He phoned her from prison, promising everything was going to be okay, keeping the air of charm. He used the moment to preach his innocence. He never wanted to let go of her and did all he could to keep her wooed. His smooth-talking way kept her heart tied to his fingertips. Her love for him kept her mind cloaked in doubt. There was no way the man who meant as much as he did to her could do these things.

On November 10, Jerry Thompson made a call to the King County Police. He had to inform them that Bundy indeed made bail, but his travel was to be restricted. He wanted to warn them of Bundy's arrival back to Washington.

It only made sense for Ted to make his way back to Seattle. That was his home and his original killing turf. He didn't have the support he wanted out in Salt Lake as he did in

Washington. Liz was eager to have him back in her life, and in early December, the police believed they'd lost her support. But the authorities made it their mission to stalk every single one of Bundy's movements, much to his annoyance. He went out of his way to make tracking himself as difficult as he could, and without the aid of Liz, the police struggled.

They tailed him for two months through the beginning of winter and into the holidays. Ted knew he was being followed and tried to keep one or two steps ahead of his watchdogs. He couldn't help but talk to them. He tried sympathizing, discussing the pressure the police must be under to follow him. But the pressure was on Ted. And it was building. His mask cracked ever so slightly, bit by bit. One night he made a display of rage for hearing the latest news story about him at a restaurant. He was pleased with the fame and sympathy of his friends, even though he couldn't move without worrying about the team of police. Their eyes glued to his every move. He would take photos of the police following him as well as write down their license plate numbers. As if he attempted to grab the reins of the situation. Let them know he wasn't afraid, but Ted was afraid.

Ted was certain that on February 23, 1976, the day he was called to court, he would be exonerated for the alleged kidnapping. There was no jury, only the swift and capable discernment of Judge Stewart M. Hanson Jr. The trial went on into the week, and Carol DaRonch was finally brought in. John O'Connell grilled the young woman, pressing into her. But she remained strong and determined that the man in front of her, Ted Bundy, was indeed the one who tried to kidnap her that horrible night. She spoke in a soft voice and recounted the details of that day. How she drove her burgundy Camaro to the mall to shop for gifts, and how under the disguise of a police officer, Bundy was able to lure her away from the mall and into his car. Her testimony was strong even though O'Connell did all he could to undermine the details of her story. He wanted to push the idea that the cops forced her into picking Bundy from the lineup, but it was of no use.

And on March 1, the words, "I find the defendant, Theodore Robert Bundy, guilty of aggravated kidnapping, a first-degree felony, as charged," were spoken by Judge Steward M. Hanson Jr., and Bundy's life would never be the same again. The news of the sentence shocked Bundy. He'd thought he had a case, and these police were fools. He then had a word with his parents before being taken away to the Salt Lake City jail. After the initial fear of being behind bars, Ted began to do well. He became the jailhouse lawyer and exchanged legal advice to other inmates in exchange for goods, specifically dope. This was to be his place of residence for the next few months, but Ted wouldn't stay still for long. That was never his nature.

But they were no fools, and Mike Fisher would continue digging into the killer's motivations and plans. He wanted to see the Volkswagen. Bundy had conveniently sold it to a teenager earlier to try and rid himself of the evidence, but the Salt Lake City police had found it. Fisher worked with them to have it brought back to Denver for further investigation. When he learned the headliner and side panels hadn't been inspected he knew then, he needed to take another look. Jerry Thompson was willing, eager for any new evidence to keep Bundy locked up. They had him as a kidnapper, now they needed to gather enough evidence to lock him up forever as a murderer.

The investigation of the car proved to be extremely productive. "A few hairs were found behind the backseat area. The side panels came out. On the passenger side window and below the weather felt that seals glass from the inside of the door we found blood... The headliners came out as the search continued with samples of hair found being photographed in place and then mounted for comparison."

Fisher did not stop with the car. He continued putting together pieces of evidence that the Utah police had gone over before. He conducted interviews and examined crime scenes; bit by bit he obtained more evidence pointing to Ted Bundy as the guilty killer.

He continued into the spring.

On March 30, 1976, Bundy once again made his way before Judge Hanson. The fear of losing some of his life to rotting in a jail cell rose through him. Tears welled in the cold killer's eyes. There was no remorse for the woman he killed nor the attempted kidnapping he was charged for. He made a plea for injustice, violently defending his innocence. But these cries fell on deaf ears. Bundy was given fifteen years of time to serve in Utah's state prison.

And in October, Mike Fisher obtained the arrest warrant for Bundy for the murder of Caryn Campbell. Ted Bundy was to be brought to Denver to stand trial. Fisher arrived at the prison to personally escort Bundy, the detective sat beside the murderer in the unmarked police car. They sped along the highway. The fear mounted in Bundy. Fisher watched, describing Bundy who: "Kept slinking down to the floor. That little bastard was very afraid of dying, but his level of fear was never as high as those unfortunate and brutalized victims."

Bundy was brought to Aspen, Colorado. His arrival was met with his immediate use of charm. He smiled and talked with the warmth he'd perfected. Even the woman remarked on how handsome he was. He came across as easy going and kind. The jailers noted how little trouble he caused and eased their apprehension of him. Due to Bundy acting as his own lawyer, he was granted favors by Judge George Lohr. He was allowed access to the courthouse library to study and prepare. Bundy spent hours studying the different maps of Aspen and memorizing the roads. He stocked up on healthy foods and practiced a disciplined work out regime. The hearing began, but his demeanor made everyone a bit too relaxed with Bundy. Mike Fisher and Jerry Thompson tried to warn the jailers of Ted, but they didn't listen. He'd already sunk his hooks into them, and their complacency became their downfall.

To Tallahassee

June 7, 1977, Judge George Lohr called for a mid-morning recess. Theodore Robert Bundy made his way inside the old library of the courthouse. He came to the second story room to read and study law books, or at least that was what everyone assumed. Bundy had other plans. Plans he'd been thoroughly preparing for. Bundy's eyes fell upon the open window. He'd practiced jumping off the top bunk of his bed, readying his ankles for the impact, mentally visualizing this escape. There was no one around to watch. All he needed to do was jump, and that was exactly what he did.

His feet met the pavement, and he ran. His legs moved across the street where he jumped a fence and continued, sprinting. He made it away from the buildings and into the thick forest. "I can still feel the jolt of hitting the ground," Ted described the escape. "I popped up and leaped across the steps in front of the courthouse and then zipped toward the prosecutor's office. Went in back of that and then down to this six-foot-high wire fence. I didn't climb it or anything. I just jumped over it and somersaulted on the other side. I ran like crazy down this alleyway behind Main Street. These two guys in the back of a restaurant looked at me kinda strange because I was runnin' full tilt right by 'em! Boom! Boom! Boom! Boom!" On his person were several layers of clothes. He needed them. Bundy had plans to escape through the Aspen mountains. If he could survive in the wilderness long enough and make his way through, then he'd be right on his way to freedom.

As his feet met the hard road and freedom was a part of Ted's life once more, the courthouse realized their fatal mistake. They'd lost him. A passerby came to the courthouse mere minutes after Bundy leapt to inform them that they'd witnessed a man jump from the second-story window. Everyone knew it was most likely Bundy, but none of them wanted to believe it was true.

The Seattle Times wrote up a story immediately. "Ted Bundy Escapes!" One hundred officers began the manhunt for the escaped felon.

Mike Fisher found out post-surgery that morning as he stirred awake. He saw the news on the television; having worked tirelessly to put Ted away for the murder of Caryn Campbell, anger filled him.

But the mountains, standing several thousand feet, were no simple, recreational hike. For Ted, the next five days wandering through the forest would prove to be mentally taxing and physically grueling. He'd lose his ability to think logically, completely consumed with the physical demands of climbing up the rocky mountain. The cold and rain set in, discouraging his attempts. He eventually found a log cabin and entered it by smashing a window. The comfort of the shelter set in. Ted immediately shed his dirty clothes. The killer stood under the roof of someone's home. He noticed the different books on the shelves as well as the *Sunset* magazines. But no maps.

Exhaustion overwhelmed him to the point he didn't even try to find food. He slipped into the master bedroom, peeled back the layer of plastic on the bed, and collapsed into a deep sleep.

He awoke in the morning. His body starved. He searched the kitchen and found saltines, canned Polish bacon, a few boxes of brown sugar, stewed tomatoes, and ravioli. He gathered a few supplies including a .22 rifle and shells, a flashlight, and a blanket. He continued on after sleeping for most of the day. He set out at midnight. But without a map, Ted would become lost. The rapid weight loss and bouts of pain from his knee and ankle that were swelling, were only the beginning of his hurdles. Delusions and hallucinations overcame him, but he was determined to return to his old life away from the police. He decided to return to the cabin and regroup, but when he returned, Bundy was horrified to find boot prints all over the cabin floor. They'd got his fingerprints. Panic filled him. He finally had had enough in the wild after the owner of the cabin chased him off with a gun, warning him about the ongoing manhunt for a serial killer. Bundy used his charm to casually walk away from the cabin's owner. He told the gun-toting cabin owner a story about being a dentist with a wife and kids. The cabin owner let him go, but he followed several hundred yards behind Bundy, who didn't want to appear rushed. Instead, Bundy plucked wildflowers to make a beautiful bouquet.

He knew then he wouldn't survive in the wilderness much longer. The pain in his left leg made it practically useless. Bundy managed to make it down to one of the main roads in Aspen by nightfall. If he wanted to get out of Colorado, he was going to have to steal a car.

He found a Cadillac. The keys had been left underneath the driver's seat. It was exactly what Ted needed. He got in, jumping on Highway 82. Real freedom was simply a drive away.

But the effects of spending days out in the wilderness had taken a drastic toll on Bundy. That Sunday morning, early in the dark of 2:00 am, Bundy barely managed to maintain control of his vehicle. He swerved along the road, exhaustion taking over.

A local patrol car took immediate note of the blue Cadillac dodging along the lanes. They assumed it was a drunk driver and began the pursuit. Their sirens wailed and caught Bundy's attention; he pulled over. Taking deep breaths, Bundy planned to play it cool and hope they let him go. He'd lost over thirty pounds during his time in the wild. His hair was scruffy and his beard out of control. One of the officers, who knew Bundy from being in the Aspen prison, immediately made the connection, but he was not sure. The officer shined the light in Bundy's eyes. More officers arrived at the scene and passersby would call out wanting to know what was unfolding. "We think we've got Bundy," they'd say back. The official truth of who'd they grabbed that night wouldn't come out until Bundy's return to Pitkin County jail. Theodore Robert Bundy was back in Aspen.

It was nothing more than a short respite of freedom.

Bundy was returned to prison, but his known freedoms were taken away. No amount of sweet-talking could win them back now. As he defended himself in court, he was locked in leg irons and chains. But even with such physical limitations, Bundy's body healed, and his need for escape never left him. The time behind bars had seemed to cleanse him of his inner demonic entity. He was ready to reinvent his identity. It was time to escape again, but he would take more time planning.

The months passed, and December came. He wouldn't be able to move forward the way he wanted to in Aspen. He was too well-known here, and he needed a change of location. Somewhere fresh, where his chances of getting an acquittal were higher. He presented himself before the judge, who listened and granted the request. Bundy would get the new setting he so desired. Pride beamed from him. He got the judge to do what he wanted, but then in a matter of minutes, the pride and joy were sucked out of Ted immediately. The judge agreed to move the trial to El Paso County. Ted turned to his attorney, questioning where this change of trial would take place, only to find out El Paso County was in Colorado Springs.

Ted Bundy was in trouble. His easy-going prison experience would quickly be replaced by the hard and tough El Paso County Jail. He wouldn't be able to escape from there. His time was limited now, and if he wanted to get back out into the world, Bundy knew he had to act quickly. He had been working on a plan for some time. With the hacksaw he received from a fellow prisoner, Bundy cut away the welds of the ceiling fixture in his cell and removed it entirely. The hole formed was a tight fit. Bundy had no choice but to starve himself, already thin from living in the wilderness for those five days, it didn't take long for his body to slim down to an appropriate size. He investigated the space above his cell, and after venturing, he'd return to his cell to pull the plate back over the hole in the ceiling. He found himself in a narrow dusty crawl space; the other prisoners heard his rustling as he moved above them. He did this several times, going a bit farther each practice only to return to his cell. He found a spot leading to a small apartment where one of the jail staff lived. This would be his path to the outside.

During this December, Ted was visited by Carol Ann Boone. They'd kept their correspondence going. With Liz on the fence, Bundy needed a replacement. Carol believed Ted and didn't think he was capable of the crimes accused. For Bundy, it was important to have some sort of companionship with a woman. Perhaps, he needed to be told that someone chose to love him and believed he was incapable of these heinous crimes.

Either way, deep down he knew his guilt and desired to escape.

New Year's Eve came. Bundy stood beside his bed, pulling the bedding over a pile of law books, clothes, and anything else he could find to fashion in the shape of a body. His goal was to fool the passive guards into believing he was doing nothing more than sleeping away the night. Earlier he'd made sure to let the guards know he was feeling under the weather. He refused food and laid in bed. They wouldn't be suspicious of the bedridden lump buried beneath blankets.

Like so many practice runs, Ted removed the fixture in the ceiling and hoisted himself up. He made his way to the small apartment. He knew the head jailer and his wife were at the movies, and the guards' minds would be on the holiday. A shining light from below stopped him. He waited, wondering if he should risk continuing. Bundy left it to chance and entered the small apartment. He switched out of his prison garb and into street clothes. He got his ticket out.

He'd done it. Bundy stepped out into the cold winter snow, able to pass by the jail under the guise of a regular citizen. The sense of elation filled him. He'd escaped a second time. With $700 in his pocket received from donations for his defense and the feeling of being unstoppable, all Bundy needed was a means to get out of this place, away from the police and detectives. A fresh start.

Also, he needed a car.

In the bitter chill air, he walked up and down the streets, looking for anyone who may have left their keys on the seat or under the visor. A quick and easy mode of transportation for him to simply drive away with. He found one after four hours. He hopped in to discover the thing had no heat, little gas, and hardly shifted gears. But the engine turned on. The falling snow thickened around him into a blizzard. Shortly, the ratty, old car gave out. The temperature was dropping quickly, and the visibility of the road was fading. He wondered if his grand escape plan would end with him frozen in a snowdrift. But for Ted, he believed this was his night. Nothing could stop him. He got out of the car and waved down a passing car. It was a kind soldier driving a Mazda, who helped Bundy push his stolen vehicle away from the road. Bundy told the kind samaritan his wife was having a baby and he needed to get to her as soon as possible. Eager to help and for the company, the soldier drove Ted to the bus station. He hopped onto a Trailways bus to Denver then took a cab to the airport.

It was 8:55 am when Ted Bundy leaned back in his seat on the plane. He ordered himself a scotch and soda then settled in.

He touched down in Chicago that morning.

Here, Ted Bundy was unknown. A shadow of nothing more than a normal man going about his life. He wanted to get as far away as possible from the West.

Bundy got a seventeen-hour head start before the guards realized how easily they'd been duped. A pile of books had tricked them all. Mike Fisher and his wife rose that morning, ready to start the New Year only to have the news of Bundy's escape jolt him out of bed. He described his emotion as "livid." In his office, Fisher slipped into a rage; a list of profanities left his mouth. No matter the hurried efforts the cops undertook in hopes to stop Ted, he was long gone and on an Amtrak train headed to Ann Arbor, Michigan.

Bundy made his way to a bar to watch the Rose Bowl game. His alma mater the University of Washington was playing the Michigan Wolverines. Surrounded by college students and other patrons, he studied the people. They were able to go home to their families, pursue careers and dreams. And even though Bundy was free from his prison, he'd never be free to live as they do. He could not return home. Never start a family. The situation he found himself in was completely out of his control. His career goals were dashed as well. All he could do now was run. Isolated and alone. The euphoria he'd found days earlier upon escaping disappeared into a vacuum of emptiness.

He'd only drank beer for about an hour, but the alcohol took its toll. Bundy stumbled into the bar's bathroom and retched. The bartender threatened to call the police.

He left the bar and walked through the cold Michigan snow to the university's library. His eyes fell to catalogs with information about colleges on the Gulf Coast. He would choose Florida State University to be his next destination. It was far enough away from his past, perhaps a new life was attainable there. The warmth and the sun would be nice, and Florida State was close enough to the ocean. Tallahassee was Bundy's new destination. He made his plan.

On Tuesday, January 3, Bundy spent most of the day walking along the sidewalks searching for a readily available car. He couldn't hot wire, so it had to be waiting for him. The cold Midwest air chewed at him. His feet were numb as he walked along the side streets and wet from the icy snow. Slipping into a darkened church, Bundy managed to steal a few hours of sleep, only to spend most of his Wednesday doing the same until his eyes fell upon an old model Japanese sedan. He found it sitting in the parking lot of a repair shop.

At 5:30 pm the sun set early into the long winter night, Ted Bundy drove out of Ann Arbor, Michigan. Without a map, he struggled to find his route, losing time, but he managed to find the freeway and headed south. He drove until the exhaustion was unbearable, and he pulled to the side of the road to sleep some more.

Bundy arrived in Tallahassee with the new name of "Chris Hagen." He situated himself in an old house in the upstairs room at 409 West College Avenue. It was a massive home full of undergraduates attending Florida State University, a member of a local rock band, a graduate student, and an ex-military man. Bundy was a bit older than most of the house's residents, but he still held up the façade that he was a law student. There was a steady stream of individuals coming and going inside the walls of their home. For Ted Bundy, this was exactly what he wanted. He could blend right in.

Some of the residents found the supposed Chris Hagen a bit off. They took note of his lack of eye contact. They noticed how he kept late hours, drank a lot, and jogged often. At times he was seen wearing glasses, but a little odd was no problem. Some people were simply like that. He seemed fine enough otherwise. For Bundy, this is exactly what he wanted. To start over as Chris in anonymity. No longer worried about the police tackling him to the ground if he was spotted. He reasoned to lay low and avoid any activity that might stir unwanted suspicion. He filled his apartment with a variety of stolen items and gathered a good amount of stolen credit cards. For Bundy, he'd rather steal than work. He'd never been one to hold down a job for long. He tried to apply for a job at a construction site, but his failure to be able to produce any identification forced him to walk away. For Bundy, stealing was easier.

And so with the start of theft, the cycle of evil Bundy had developed over his life began again. He slipped into the well of madness, and it was only a matter of time for the monster to take control once more. Bundy's life wasn't headed in the direction he wanted. It had been a long while since he'd stolen the breath of a young woman. His need was violent and desperate.

He was no longer capable of the smooth-talking, charming allure. His violent sexual urges consumed him.

Saturday, January 14, 1978, Bundy recalled that he was fairly certain he spent his evening alone in his room. Though he couldn't recall all the details, many remember the night quite differently.

In a report filed with the Florida State University Police, Cheryl Rafferty was a student almost abducted by a man of Bundy's appearance and size. She had gotten out of her car and was making her way to the dorm. A man leapt from the bushes and approached her with startling speed. Cheryl was frightened, her pace quickened as did the man's. Her walk turned into a sprint, but she managed to enter Reynolds Hall.

This occurred five hours before Ted Bundy entered Chi Omega.

He was seen peering in through windows of apartments and houses along West Pensacola Avenue. The hours began to creep by, and Bundy had yet to find his next possession. He left the streets and entered the bar Sherrod's, the disco next door to Chi Omega. Around midnight, the disheveled killer made his way in. But his strange state of behavior was noticed. He was bursting at the seams. His cool composure was long gone. This was no longer Ted Bundy; this was a beast hungry to inflict pain.

He breathed heavily, paced, and acted strangely. Two students, Carla Jean Black and Valerie Stone entered the disco. Valerie Stone went to order a drink at the bar. But she couldn't help but notice the strange man. He didn't match the aesthetic of a college student. She thought he looked greasy and too old. But what bothered her the most was the way he just stared at her. She worried he planned to ask for a dance.

Next door from Sherrod's at Chi Omega, Kathy Kleinar and Karen Chandler were in bed on the second floor, room eight around midnight. Kathy had spent the evening with her fiancé, and Karen made dinner for her mother who was battling the flu. And across the hall was room number four, where Lisa Levy shared a room with Debra O'Brien. Earlier that night Lisa had been at the bar Sherrod's, but she grew rather bored of the disco. When none of her friends wanted to change locations and try somewhere else she decided to call it a night and wound back home in her sweats watching television by 11:30 pm. She'd planned to be at church tomorrow morning with friends.

In room number nine, Margaret Bowman stayed. But her roommate was out of town for the weekend. Margaret had a date earlier that night. The fraternity brother wanted to coax her into staying out later with him, but she declined, dropped him off, and returned home for bed. That was around 2:00 am when Melanie Nelson came back from Sherrod's that evening with Leslie Waddel and a male friend. They were surprised to find the back door ajar, letting in the cool winter air, but that was normal with the constant stream of people coming and going. Melanie was sure to lock it then.

She found Margaret upstairs, undressing, and preparing for bed. Leslie Waddel and her friend were hungry. They asked Margaret if she wanted to get some hamburgers. Margaret, tired from her date, declined, but she offered them her car. Melanie Nelson lingered for a bit, talking about Margaret's date in detail and how fun it was. They spoke for a while.

During this time Nancy Dowdy and Terri Murphy came home. It was around 2:35 am. Both found the glass sliding door secured and locked.

Five minutes later, Melanie Nelson said goodnight to Margaret Bowman and went to her room. Nothing felt out of the ordinary.

Carol Johnston returned home at 3:00 am. She noticed the glass sliding door was open. The upstairs hallway lights were off. This was unusual. Before finding her way to her bed in room two, across from Margaret's, Carol went to the bathroom. Because it was late and she was tired, she left the door open.

Click.

A doorknob turned. She figured it was one of the other girls moving through the house. She went to her room. The digital clock read 3:14 am when she turned off the lights to go to sleep.

Ted Bundy stood outside; it was doubtful he'd put much planning into the night. After an unsuccessful time at Sherrod's he made his way to Chi O. Perhaps the sorority girls attending the disco that night inspired his attack. Either way, he would have waited outside, realizing the back sliding glass door was the perfect entry. He wouldn't search long for a weapon, choosing the heavy oak log from a woodpile and wrapped it in cloth.

He might have slipped in immediately after Carol, not waiting a moment to rush the first bedroom. The click she heard could have been Ted creeping in after his initial attack. Experts believe Lisa Levy might have been his first violent visit. Bundy entered Lisa's room and savagely attacked her. She was horribly beaten but died from strangulation. In Lisa's state of near-death or in death, Bundy tore into her buttocks, sinking his teeth deep in and leaving a bite mark. He ripped her right nipple off as well in the state of animalistic rage.

He most likely moved then to Kathy Kleinar and Karen Chandler's shared room. Lisa Levy's blood type was found on their walls and ceiling splattered about where he clubbed them both, smashing their heads and breaking their jaws. There was no time to react as they were fast asleep when the possessed monster violently attacked them. Fear filled the two girls. They couldn't process the nightmarish situation, only suffer in the confusion as the pain overcame them.

Bundy slipped out of Kathy and Karen's room and most likely went to Bowman next. He strangled her with a pair of pantyhose tightly around her neck. At some point she'd received a crushing blow to her head and when her body was found it was still warm.

It was during this brutal attack Nita Neary kissed her date goodbye and entered Chi Omega to find the horror that awaited her. Perhaps it was the sound of Nita downstairs moving about that stopped Bundy, but he made a run for it after his quick attack. Like a hurricane of pain and fear that swept through the sorority, he raced down the stairs, most likely unaware of Nita who stood frozen in fear. The young woman caught the shadowed image of a strange man clutching a heavy club in his hand.

Nita Neary coming home to the slaughterhouse left behind by Bundy did not mean he was finished. His thirst for violence and sex was awakened, and his trail of terror propelled him forward. In his hand he continued gripping the club, now dripping with the blood of his most recent victims. But Bundy wasn't satiated quite yet. He still had more use for the murderous hunk of wood. In a dazed state of bloodlust, he continued on down the street.

He stopped at 431-A Dunwoody Street where his next victim slept peacefully. It was 4:00 am when Bundy entered the older duplex. With the log he used on the Chi Omega girls, he entered the bedroom of Cheryl Thompson still in a state of anger and rage. With incredible force sheerly driven by animalistic rage and the entity, Bundy hammered Cheryl's jaw and head with several crushing blows. Thompson cried out in fear and pain. Her friends who shared the other side of the duplex awoke from the sounds of terror. Debbie Ciccarelli, one of the roommates, was yanked from her sleep. "I woke up to this loud pounding... It was just a real loud banging sound... We could hear Cheryl moaning, whimpering. I called Cheryl. We could hear the phone ringing because the wall was so thin, but she wasn't answering her phone," she said. She and her roommate called out for Cheryl but heard no response, only the sound of footsteps.

Those footsteps belonged to a murderer trespassing in the night. Bundy was moving now, removing his pants to continue the lust-driven anger. He planned to have anal intercourse with her as he killed her with the pantyhose he clutched. The sensation of taking a life amplified his sexual experience. But the sounds of the neighbors calling out took away this twisted relief. There was no time. He finished by masturbating, leaving a bloody and broken Cheryl Thompson, whose housemates had managed to call the police at this time. He escaped through the window from which he arrived and disappeared into the night.

Within minutes the police were on the scene. They found Cheryl. Half-conscious moans of pain escaping her throat. Blood dripped from the wounds. To the police, it was painfully clear the man who visited Cheryl had been the same one who visited Chi Omega minutes before. Cheryl would live but suffer permanent hearing loss as well as the loss of balance.

His night was over.

Bundy returned home to his apartment. He stood out in front of the home in the cool Florida winter air. He did not return the greetings of the other residents. He was lost to the world, consumed by his inner monster. Russell Gage and Henry Palumbo returned to the house they shared with Bundy around 4:00 am. They saw the man they knew as Chris.

He stood out in front of the porch with a blank expression across his face. He did not greet them. But after a short while, he made his way back into the home to discuss the Chi Omega murders with other residents who were still awake at the time. The news of the violent attacks played over the radio. Bundy listened and then said, "This was probably a professional job, and this guy has done it before."

But the news of the murders shook the city. Bundy found some delight knowing he incited the fear taking hold. He engaged in conversations about the murders with other residents. Even giddy with delight assuming he escaped with another successful string of murders and attacks, he commented about how smart it was that the killer used a weapon that couldn't be traced. No one from the residence recalled the news releasing information about the weapon.

Little did he realize, Bundy robbed himself of a potentially normal life.

But Bundy would still try. He managed to survive off stolen credit cards, continuing to prey on the kindness of others. He got his hands on a duplicate of Kenneth Raymond Misner's birth certificate. Misner was popular, a former track star and student at Florida State University. Bundy knew enough details to get by. To validate his new identity further, he had plans to get a driver's license. If he could pass under this new guise, then the man known as Ted Bundy would be another step closer to disappearing. He would only exist in the frightful memories of the people on the West Coast.

Unfortunately for Bundy, he was unable to accept a normal life. Ted needed a new kill, and he knew he'd have to put some distance between himself and the police. By February 6, 1978, Tallahassee authorities tirelessly worked to hunt the man Nita Neary saw crouching underneath her door that horrible night. Ted Bundy attempted to run away as he hopped onto I-10, heading east. He'd stolen the FSU media center van, having taken the set of keys and made a copy for himself.

The need for murder rose within him that following Monday. He began to prowl. Tuesday, he continued his hunt by driving along the highway searching with an aching hunger. He'd lost complete control over the monster inside. Now, it controlled him. But once again he failed to obtain a new victim. The monster went unfed. Defeated and empty-handed, he stayed the night at a Holiday Inn under a fake name paying with a stolen credit card.

The next day came. In a K-Mart shopping center parking lot, he stopped the van. It was not by chance he'd found a spot across from a junior high school. Here he struck up a conversation with Leslie Ann Parmenter. She was only fourteen at the time. The young woman looked upon what she would describe as an unkempt, messy man, who was agitated. She described him as "real fidgety, digging in his pockets like he didn't know what he was going to say next or anything, like he was unsure of himself."

He got out of the van, leaving the driver's side door open. He carried a plastic fireman's badges with the name Richard Burton pinned on his coat. It was most likely a cheap costume piece.

Suspicion poured through Leslie. She was unsure what the strange man wanted. Her older brother arrived just in time then. He pulled up in his truck. Her brother asked Bundy what he wanted. There was no reason for such an older man, a complete stranger even, to be striking up a conversation with his younger sister. He wanted to know what Bundy was after and why he needed to speak with Leslie. Nervous and uncomfortable, Bundy pulled together a lie, weakly stating he thought Leslie could have been someone else. Her brother caught on to Bundy's nerves. Making the correct decision and possibly saving Leslie's life, her brother instructed Leslie to get into his truck. "He was very nervous... Like he was almost shaking. His voice was even quivering," her brother recalled.

But to Bundy, losing his prey was irritating. He was unhappy. Crack. His mask continued to weaken and splinter. He was losing his grip entirely. He continued on, driving. He stopped that night at a Holiday Inn along the road. He booked the room under the name Ralph Miller. He had dinner and a few drinks at the hotel bar, but he did not sit there unnoticed. A few of the patrons could not help but remember the disturbed looking man with greasy dark and dirty hair. They noted something was off about the stranger. He was weird. One witness described Bundy as, "He looked either drunk or spaced out, he acted funny, slurred his words [and] his clothes were rough."

A cold rain came in the morning as Bundy awoke. He drove a ways until he came to Lake City Junior High School. He circled around the school. He'd had luck before with junior high schools. These girls were easy targets for him. Young and trusting, they were taught to listen to adults. Most had the children's best interest at heart.

Not Ted Bundy.

Twelve-year-old Kimberly Leach was leaving to retrieve the purse she left behind. Her thoughts were on the upcoming school's Valentine dance and the new dress she wanted to wear. She was moving between the portable and the school's main building. Without a breath of hesitation, Bundy whipped the van to the side of the road, lunged out, and snatched the twelve-year-old girl.

The mask cracked completely. The man inside was no longer there. There was no guise to lure the lamb to the slaughter. He had no story. No lies to reel the child into his clutches. He was so desperate to feed the monster inside any rationale left his mind. The demon was hungry.

C.L. Anderson, a former firefighter, observed someone who looked similar to Bundy grabbing the arm of a crying young girl. Later in a court testimony, Anderson described what he saw. He noticed a man was angry, dragging the girl to the passenger door. He shoved her in. Anderson thought it was nothing more than a father dealing with a temper tantrum. It would take him six months before he told anyone what he saw that day.

With his new possession, Bundy sped away in the white, stolen van. He nearly ran a woman off the road. His mind was lost in a sea of evil desires taking hold. Kimberly Leach's fight would have ended quickly after entering the van. Bundy most likely knocked her unconscious. But he knew if he wanted to carry through his acts of sexual violence he would need to stop soon. It was far too risky driving on the highway with a young victim.

He drove to a more rural area and during this point he raped Kimberly but did not kill her. Not yet. He was working on the fly and did not have a premeditated location to commit his crimes as he had in Washington. Instead, he found an empty, cramped hog shed. Under the metal-roofed, small structure, Bundy dragged Kimberly Leach inside. A knife rested in the palm of his hand. He forced Kimberly to lie down on her stomach. Then he had sex with her once more, and in the act he stabbed her, slashing her throat. She died immediately.

When it was over, Bundy was finally relieved of the beast rising in him. He was ready to return to Tallahassee. Close to the city limits, Bundy found a place to dump the van. Beforehand, he made sure to meticulously wipe down any area fingerprints might be found.

The evening after Bundy came back to Tallahassee, he had made plans with one of the other residents of the home he rented. They got dinner together, generously purchased with one of Bundy's stolen credit cards. The two had hit it off quite well, and Bundy was enjoying the success of his kill. But at the same time, Bundy's life in Tallahassee would have to come to an end.

Two weeks after the Chi Omega killings, Robert Keppel heard the news. He made a direct call to the Tallahassee authorities. In the conversation, he told them all about Theodore Robert Bundy. The cold killer with an insatiable appetite for young beautiful college co-eds. Mike Fisher would also make a call to inform them of Ted. They were closing in.

But Bundy, being aware that his time in Tallahassee needed to come to a close, began plans to escape from the city. If he had left earlier, he may have escaped authorities once more, but it wasn't until February 10, 1978, when Bundy decided to leave. His plan began as always, walking along the streets looking for the next unguarded vehicle. He found a green '75

Toyota, with its keys still in the ignition. Without a second thought, he pulled away in the car. It was his now. That evening, he concluded with having dinner again with the same resident. They watched television together, chatting away. She was completely unaware that the man she sat beside was not Chris Hagen nor a law student. When they were finished, he left the house and began to wander looking for something to steal.

One officer, parked in his unmarked police car would take note of the man creeping along the line of houses. Bundy immediately saw the officer and took evasive measures. He slipped away and returned home. For Bundy, it was clearly time to leave.

He began to pack the stolen Toyota around 1:00 am, Officer Dawes noticed the strange behavior. It wasn't that Bundy was doing anything particularly wrong. The officer simply knew that during hours like these, people were usually up to no good. He approached Bundy inquiring about his late-night activities. Bundy kept his composure as Dawes hopped out of his cruiser and asked Bundy for identification. Coolly, Bundy let him know he didn't have any on his person. "Where do you live?" Dawes asked. Without thinking much, Bundy blurted out "College Avenue."

Dawes peered into the car with his flashlight. It lit up the license plate sitting in the car. Bundy mentioned then that he'd merely found the plate. Dawes returned to his vehicle. He planned to call in both the plates of the Toyota as well as the one sitting on the seat, which belonged to the van Bundy had stolen earlier. He reached for his radio, only to find that Bundy had taken off into the night, sprinting away. By now, Dawes understood a chase would be useless. Instead, the stolen car and items were immediately impounded.

Bundy returned to his room. He sat with the lights off, staring out the window. He was waiting. Waiting for nothing. Tomorrow, he decided he would leave Tallahassee for good.

But tomorrow was not Ted Bundy's day.

February 12, Bundy stood outside a Mormon church. The first thing on his list was to obtain another vehicle. His Toyota had been impounded, but it was no matter. His eyes fell on the keys hanging in the ignition of a Mazda. He hopped in, turned it on, only to find the car was in horrible shape. It would never make the journey Bundy needed. He drove it a few blocks, only to decide to dump it.

Bundy was losing time. His plan of escape that morning was eluding him. But there was a twist of luck. In the same location he dumped the Mazda, fate led him to a Volkswagen Beetle. The same year as the one he used to own, a '68. There the keys sat as if they were meant for Ted to take. He got in and a sort of nostalgic feeling came over him. He could tell someone put a lot of money and time into the car. He couldn't take it. As if, suddenly Ted was hit with a sense of morals. He got out and finally settled on a beat-up, orange 1972 Volkswagen Beetle. It was about 11:00 pm when Bundy finally drove away from

Tallahassee, onward to the next city. The next place he could leave a cold-blooded trail.

Or at least he thought.

Bundy's time was at an end.

Monster Caged

Wednesday, February 15, Bundy should have been long out of Florida. He'd spent several days on the road, trying to get by. He showered in the airport and used stolen credit cards for food. He'd slept in the VW. His last day of freedom ended with him drunk in a bar. He'd planned to nab several wallets to help him get by, but he was caught rifling through a purse and kicked out.

And now at 1:30 am, he drove fairly drunk down the freeway. This caught the immediate attention of Pensacola patrolman David Lee.

David Lee turned on his flashing lights and pulled Bundy over. Lee called in the plate numbers to find out that this was a stolen vehicle. He withdrew his revolver and ordered Bundy to exit the car and lay face down on the road. Bundy did as he was told. His nose pressed against the pavement. The patrolman asked if there was anyone else, lingering in the vehicle. Bundy did not answer, and suddenly the hard reality of cold metal handcuffs came down upon his left wrist. If Bundy wanted to escape, he would have to do it now.

Bundy flipped over onto his back, striking Lee before the other cuff made it on his right wrist. Lee lost his balance, and Ted seized the opportunity. The murderer took the officer's legs out from under him. Bundy lunged forward at the patrolman.

Lee fired.

But the bullet missed. Bundy was quick, running for his life. He pivoted on his feet then bolted away. Lee stayed close to the perpetrator's heels chasing after the murderer.

Lee, having no handcuffs nor back up if this criminal was armed, took no chances; he lifted his revolver and aimed once more. The gun went off and this time the man fell flat on the ground. He'd hit, or at least he'd thought so.

Lee approached, but an unharmed Bundy once again kicked at Lee's leg. Instead of running, Bundy jerked forward attempting to snatch the gun from the officer, who was not about to let go. The two engaged with one another. Bundy screamed for help, alerting the nearby homeowners. The onlookers realized the situation at hand and refrained from helping. With the heavy barrel of his gun, Lee hit Bundy three times in the face. Bloodied and now beaten, Bundy fell back. He could not fight, and he was promptly taken into custody.

He kept up a charade, giving the authorities a false name. But as they dug deeper, the devastating truth of who this deranged criminal was slowly emerged.

He finally agreed to reveal his name after working out a deal to secure an attorney. They were stunned to find out sitting in front of them was none other than Theodore Robert Bundy. The man, who from the hard-won efforts of Mike Fisher, had just landed a spot on the FBI's Most Wanted. As part of the deal, he was allowed to use the prison telephone for two hours. He reached out to Liz.

During this state of emotional and physical exhaustion, Bundy began to confess. Perhaps he was too broken to care, but when he spoke to Liz, pieces of the story began to fall out. Some pieces he would later regret divulging. But Bundy did not want to discuss the Chi Omega killings nor Kimberly Leach. He avoided these topics refusing to give in.

His confession to Elizabeth would ultimately be their end.

For the Florida authorities, all they wanted was to coax Bundy into admitting he was indeed the murderer they knew he was. For Bundy, knowing he was to be locked up, he wanted to bargain a return to Washington. He wanted to get out of Florida. If the police wanted information on the killings he could play his cards right to secure the move. But as Ted tried to bait them with information, Florida had no intention of letting Bundy go.

They found Kimberly's body on April 7. Florida was now one step closer to ending Bundy.

He was shortly brought to trial. Bundy was overwhelmed with the attention. The world was suddenly his. People were listening to him, watching his every move. He basked in the glory of it. Even if the glory was him walking right into his own grave.

With the two years of law school under his belt, Bundy's hubris led him to believe he could handle his own defense. His arrogance blinded him, painfully. He had completely disassociated himself from the horrible crimes committed at his hands. There was no guilt. Bundy had excellent legal defense and assistance from Millard Farmer and Mike Minerva, but he rarely relied on their expertise, choosing to trust in himself. Unknowingly, the mistakes he would go on to make would only help the Floridan authorities. It was as if Ted was determined to fight himself.

July 27, 1978, Ted Bundy was read the indictments for Chi Omega and shortly then for the Kimberly Leach murder.

During the two trials in Florida, Bundy ignored the legal advice provided. When offered by his legal team the idea of claiming insanity, he immediately rejected it. Having sex with the dead and removing his victims' heads as trophies was not—

to Bundy—grounds for insanity. He diminished these acts as nothing more than "my problem" or "acting out."

Finally, in April of 1979, Bundy's team agreed to a plea deal. If Ted Bundy confessed to the Chi Omega and Kimberly Leach murders, he would then be spared the death sentence. Instead, he'd serve three life sentences locked away in jail. His love at the time, Carol Ann Boone, wanted him to desperately take the deal to ensure his life. Pride got in the way. Bundy struggled with accepting the plea deal. Some part of him couldn't do it. In the end, he signed the agreement.

The day in court came for Bundy to admit guilt. He held the confession in his hand and the whole courtroom fell silent, eager to hear him confess. But instead, Bundy attacked his defense team. He claimed they were overwhelmed and underprepared. "Your Honor," Ted went on, glorying in the spotlight, "it is not simply my point of view that I'm not receiving effectiveness of counsel. It is my position that my counsel, one, believe that I'm guilty; two, that they have told me they see no way of presenting an effective defense, and in no uncertain terms they have told me that; and three, that they see no way of avoiding conviction. Now, Your Honor, if this doesn't raise itself to the level of ineffectiveness of counsel, I don't know what does."

Perhaps Bundy felt proud rejecting the plea, but the false sense of victory was short-lived. One of his lawyers approached him during a short called recess. "Well, Ted," said Farmer, "we really gave it a try here. I've got no hard feelings, but I've only got so much time and I'm going to spend it on people who want to live."

It was clear the evidence against Bundy was strong. Nita Neary had no problem identifying the man she saw in the knit cap and navy peacoat lurking in the sorority that night. The bite marks left on Lisa Levy were almost irrefutable. And on July 23, the jury found Theodore Robert Bundy guilty of the Chi Omega murders.

Bundy could not believe it. He was taken aback as he heard the sentence. He looked up at the judge and said, "I find it somewhat absurd to ask for mercy for something I did not do, so I will be tortured for, and suffer for, and receive the pain for the act. But I will not share the burden of the guilt."

For these murders, Bundy was sentenced to a swift death by electric chair. But the Judge gave Bundy a few parting words.

Take care of yourself, young man. Take care of yourself. I say that to you sincerely. It's a tragedy to this court to see such a total waste of humanity. You're a bright young man. You'd have made a good lawyer. And I'd have loved to have you practice in front of me. I bear you no animosity, believe me. But you went the other way, partner. Take care of yourself.

The second trial was moved to Orlando for the murder of Kimberly Leach. The trial began on January 7, 1980. This time,

Bundy was not as eager to jump in front of the cameras nor undermine his legal team. He kept Carol close to him and continued to deny the guilt, but even then, the weight of it all bore down upon him.

The amount of evidence against Bundy was powerful. Leslie Parmenter, whose older brother came to the rescue and recorded the license plate of the stolen van, positively identified Bundy. Deputy Dawes identified Bundy as the man who ran off into the night as he called in that stolen license plate.

The evidence continued to grow. The credit cards placed him at the location along the murder timelines. And C.L. Anderson, the retired firefighter, knew it was Bundy who grabbed the arm of the young, helpless Kimberly Leach. Even with the eye-witness verification, a fiber was found in the white stolen van. The fibers of the van matched the fiber found on Kimberly Leach's clothes.

On February 6, 1980, the jury acted according to the mounting evidence. Bundy was guilty. Then three days later, during the conclusion of the Leach trial, Carol was brought in as a character witness. As she was on the stand, Bundy asked Carol to be his wife. She accepted. According to the Floridian laws of the time, a marriage proposal on the floor of the courtroom meant the couple was automatically and legally married. Ted Bundy and Carol exchanged vows to be married during his defense.

No one knows exactly why he did this. Perhaps it was a way to celebrate a moment in his life, for two years to the day of February 9, was the day Bundy raced away with Kimberly to murder her.

With time running out, Bundy knew his death was evident and near. He reached out to Mike Fisher. He planned to buy himself time by revealing the details of the murders and to answer questions while on death row. He spoke about some of the Colorado murders but not all. Not until the day of his execution as he was led to the electric chair. His head already shaved. He asked for a tape recorder. While sitting down he told the details of two more murders. He'd spent his nine years in prison with countless interviews. He'd lost some sense of self and had become more or less a shell of the man he once was. Carol had left him. His confession was too difficult for her to deal with, but he spoke with his mother, apologizing, and attempting to explain why he did what he had.

But his time came, and he was brought to the chair on January 24, 1989. His last words were those of "love to my family and friends." At 7:06 am, 2,000 volts of electricity were shot through Bundy's body. His fists clenched once then twice. A minute of pure shock tore through him. When it was over, the black hood covering his face was pulled back. The witnesses remained silent as those piercing blue eyes, half-opened, stared at nothing. Bundy had served his sentence for the death of Kimberly Leach. He was never convicted for the murders in Washington, Utah, or Colorado.

At 7:10 am, Theodore Robert Bundy was pronounced dead.

Printed in Dunstable, United Kingdom

65500603R10119